The New Book of Gymnastics

The New Book of Gymnastics

Meg Warren

Arthur Barker Limited   London
A subsidiary of Weidenfeld (Publishers) Limited

Published in Great Britain by Arthur Barker Limited
91 Clapham High Street, London SW4 7TA

ISBN 0 213 16772 7 (Cased)
ISBN 0 213 16773 5 (Paperback)
Set, printed and bound in Great Britain by
Fakenham Press Limited, Fakenham, Norfolk

Acknowledgements

The photographs in this book are reproduced by
kind permission of the following:
Alan E. Burrows: *cover, frontispiece*, 13 *above*, 13
above right, 21 *left*, 21 *below left*, 29 *above*, 43, 46, 55,
65, 77, 79 *left*, 93 *above*, 93 *left*, 99, 109, 113
Eileen Langsley: 13 *right*, 21 *below*, 29 *below*, 37, 47
Jim Prestidge: 79 *above*, 93 *above left*

Contents

Preface

Since I wrote *The Book of Gymnastics* nearly ten years ago the sport of gymnastics has become more widely known than its educational counterpart.

Modern educational gymnastics as taught in schools and Olympic or artistic gymnastics are not the same. In the former a child is given the opportunity to work within a task to his or her own level, whereas artistic gymnastics is taught through increased body preparation and training, leading to improved technique.

Many school teachers and other enthusiasts are now finding themselves becoming involved in the sport of gymnastics without very much in the way of formal training. *The New Book of Gymnastics* provides a comprehensive teaching handbook which will aid both pupil and teacher to higher standards and will indicate the type of coaching skills normally learnt on courses. However, from the coach's point of view, this book must not be treated as a substitute for formal training or for learning through observation of individual gymnasts.

In this completely revised edition the first chapter on warm-up and body preparation has been greatly expanded; the potential gymnast and coach must understand that this aspect is a vital part of gymnastics from the beginning if success and safety are to be enjoyed. The other chapters are devoted to perfecting skills on the Olympic Four: floor, vault, beam and bars. The use of training apparatus is described in the relevant sections.

Meg Warren
December 1979

Introduction

Gymnastics is a sport requiring strength and mobility, grace and poise, courage and dedication. All these qualities are rarely found in the would-be gymnast. If the whole range of gymnastics is to be covered, these qualities must be trained and implanted in the gymnast.

The standards achieved in gymnastics can vary enormously. In this book I have tried to cover basic skills leading to those which are more advanced, stressing the high quality needed for perfection. Obviously I would like to think that every coach and gymnast should and would be capable of taking up these high ideals, but for any amount of reasons this may not be possible.

As a coach it is essential that you learn all the time. I believe that you will improve your knowledge if you use this book correctly but you will also need to attend coaching courses and visit other gym clubs. Refer to this book from time to time but do not be afraid of thinking things out for yourself and perhaps coming to your own conclusions; listen to as many good coaches as possible, watch films, television and competitions, anything that will improve your knowledge of this complex sport.

There are some standards other than technical ones that can be and should be achieved by all, coach and gymnast alike. They come under the following heading.

Responsibilities of coach and gymnast

Gymnastic dress

Whenever possible the gymnast should wear a one piece costume known as a leotard. This is the required costume for competitions. It should be well fitting but not so tight or made of hard fabric that it becomes difficult to move. They are usually made of nylon jersey and are therefore very easy to wash after wearing. They should neither be so briefly cut that the gymnast is indecent nor should they be so badly cut that the leg-holes hang towards the knees. A gymnast needs to show a good line; her garment should aid rather than hinder this. Knickers may be worn under the leotard but they must not show at any time. Young girls should not wear vests as these usually show. Girls who have reached puberty should wear well supporting bras.

Many gymnasts wear footless tights during training; a leotard only is allowed in competition. Tracksuits are also worn, particularly at the start of a training session and in a cold gym. Gymnasts' feet should be kept warm at all times so thick socks are often worn, although these must be removed or covered when vaulting or on a slippery surface. Plimsoles are not good as they are too heavy and clumsy; soft gymnastic shoes are best.

As well as the gymnast being neatly turned out at all times it is essential that the coach sets a high standard. She should always be dressed in a tracksuit or similar wear and never in jeans and a jumper.

For both coach and gymnast hair should be tied back and out of the way. Jewellery should not be worn in the gym; this point is often neglected by the coaches. Large rings and even wrist-watches can injure the gymnast whilst 'spotting' or standing in, and so can long finger-nails.

The coach

The role of the coach is very important: the standard and discipline of the gymnast is a reflection of the coach.

For any coach, whether or not her gymnasts are of high quality, intending to enter competitions or just keeping fit, the first concern must be for safety. In the first instance she must make sure that all the apparatus is properly set up and that none of it is broken. Sufficient matting must be placed round and underneath all the apparatus. Matting of varying depths or gaps where matting is meant to be joined are very dangerous.

The next safety point is a little more subtle than the former but lack of understanding about it can be very harmful. The gymnast's understanding and respect for the coach is often very great, so much so that she may attempt anything that the coach suggests. This is where the danger lies. Movements are often attempted in competition that the gymnast has no reason to be attempting as they are beyond her capabilities. This bad choice of skills reflects upon the coach, but if anybody is going to suffer it is usually the gymnast: she is the one who falls when out of control.

It is very wrong for coaches to put gymnasts in this position. They must think for the future and not for the glory of the moment.

A third point concerning safety involves preparation by way of a 'warm-up' (see page 11). The coach must always take a warm-up to ensure that all gymnasts are warm enough and supple enough to perform extreme movements such as splits without tearing or straining a muscle.

Whether gymnasts are aiming at competition or recreation the coach must teach all with one goal in mind: to make them physically fit in order that they will be able to carry themselves well, to walk, run, jump and land with ease and fluidity.

For teaching the purely recreational gymnast, there are three main points for the coach to remember: safety, physical fitness and enjoyment. Safety has already been dealt with.

Physical fitness for the recreational gymnast may be gained primarily in the warm-up session. With a large class the warm-up/body preparation is the most convenient time to teach and correct basic body positions. Work on the apparatus should be an extension of skills learnt on the floor.

For the gymnast's enjoyment she must have variety. The coach must be willing to show interest by giving praise when it is earned (not necessarily for a perfected movement but for improving on previous attempts) and by offering constructive criticism when needed. There must be a certain amount of challenge to the class or group. This may be through something daring which is within their grasp but needs a little more courage than usual, or through more skilful and intricate movements leading to more advanced exercises.

For the competitive gymnast the aims are the same but there is a different approach. Safety must be borne in mind and the coach must always consider whether the gymnast is ready to attempt a more advanced move. If she is confident that the gymnast is able to perform a somersault on her own then this will instil confidence and add to her safety. If the coach is nervous of the gymnast's ability then this nervousness will be communicated to the gymnast.

Enjoyment for this type of gymnast will come from hard work, competition, learning new movements and failure and success. If she is not prepared to work hard, is not prepared to suffer some failures, a few knocks, weary muscles and harsh words from the coach, then she is not the type of girl who will eventually become a champion gymnast.

The gymnast

The coach has a duty to the gymnast and similarly the gymnast to the coach. The gymnast must respect the coach and work for her and with her. A great deal of effort is put into the making of the gymnast by the coach, but to complete this process the gymnast must co-operate. She must always work to her maximum, giving her best at all times.

If a competitive gymnast wishes to change a movement in her voluntary exercise she must first ask her coach. A good coach should know what work her gymnasts are doing, but she will be unable to do so if one or two of them change their work when and as they wish. At the same time, work that is set by the coach for the gymnast to do on her own, either in the gym or at home, must be done conscientiously. The gymnast should also be punctual at all training sessions.

These points concerning the gymnast come under one main heading: *discipline*. Although discipline concerns the gymnast it is maintained by the coach and it is through her that discipline or lack of it exists. Discipline is what gymnastics is all about. It is I think the most highly disciplined sport currently practised. To reach the top tremendous discipline has to be maintained by the coach and self-discipline on the part of the gymnast.

The gymnast's curriculum and basic training

The human body was not made to stand in an inverted position or to make a complete turn in the air but, with training, it is very capable of doing both these things and many more movements requiring great skill.

Every normal-bodied person has potential as a gymnast; anyone can train their body to do some gymnastic skill. This may require very little training for some people, but with others a great deal more is necessary. The gymnast *must* be mobile; the muscles that restrict movements round the joints can be trained to relax more, thus allowing greater movement. The gymnast must be strong, able to support her own weight in various positions. Strength can be increased; spring, co-ordination and timing can be improved through repetition and breakdown of every movement.

Body training is usually done at the start of the training period, and then again at the end in the form of strength, endurance and mobility training. The first part of the lesson is called the 'warm-up' – a rather confusing term. Warming of the body takes very little time; it simply increases blood circulation. Any running activity can be a warm-up. However, usually included under this heading are preparatory exercises of suppling, body awareness and control. The following plan may be treated as a guide:

1 Warm-up	Physiological
	Body training: suppling exercises
	Ballet
	Basic skills
2 Class activity	Skills taught en masse
3 Apparatus	Olympic Four
	Improvised apparatus
	Vaulting and floorwork
4 Body conditioning	Strengthening
	Tension
	Endurance
	Extreme Mobility
5 Conclusion	Gymnasts line up

The time spent on sections 1–4 will vary according to the ability of the class and their gymnastic aim. On nearly every occasion, however, the warm-up should be at least twenty minutes; it may be made longer for beginners by spending less time on apparatus and a greater amount of time on body conditioning. If this is done over some time, say six months, it will be found that on the introduction of more advanced skills, training or apparatus work results will be achieved more quickly and with greater success. This could apply to any age group from eight years upwards. I have found that children under eight years, unless very exceptional, are not able to sustain concentration for long enough periods to gain rapidly from intensive training; they are more suited to general activities.

It is useful to line up the gymnasts at the end of each training session. This is a time when messages can be given out and praise or otherwise given to the class.

on the degree of tension shown. As soon as the gymnast hollows her back she should be lowered.

7 From shoulder stand the gymnast lowers her body slowly (fig. 52c), keeping it straight all the way. A partner holds the gymnast's hands down on the floor.

Mobility

For some gymnasts more time needs to be spent on mobility. It is often the case that the stiff gymnast is stronger than the supple gymnast so time could be taken out of her strengthening period. The coach may need to assist the gymnast in some of these suppling exercises. With increased mobility gymnastic skills become easier and rely more on good technique than on strength. The supple gymnast often looks more graceful and elegant so it is important for the gymnast to acquire this quality.

Exercises for extreme mobility

1 The range of movement can be increased in the splits by placing the front leg on a raised platform (fig. 53). This can also be done for the back leg.

2 The gymnast lies on her back and the coach pushes her leg close to her face (fig. 54). The gymnast pushes the leg back towards the coach as she eases the pressure. She should then relax as the coach applies pressure again. The range of movement invariably increases.

3 Using a beam or similar object the gymnast can slide her heel further from the supporting leg (fig. 55). The gymnast can also turn to face the supporting leg so that the other leg is extended backwards.

4 Using wall bars the gymnast can increase her range of movement in the pike position (fig. 56). The gymnast must put her hands over the top of the bar. By holding lower down the pull is increased. This exercise can also be done with the legs apart.

By increasing the range of movement in the shoulders the gymnast can improve her bridge position. Many gymnasts suffer from stiff backs and it is almost impossible to loosen them, so work must be done on the shoulders. Results are slow in loosening shoulders, but the following two exercises can help; exercise no. 6 is particularly effective.

5 The gymnast holds a towel or a stick and circles the arms backwards over the head (fig. 57). To increase mobility the hands should be put closer together.

6 If a gymnast cannot rest her arms on the floor when her knees are up to her chest, she should lie on the bench and continually bounce the arms downwards (fig. 58). This position must be used to ensure she does not hollow the back.

Additional exercises for strength, endurance, tension and extreme mobility can be obtained from the BAGA.

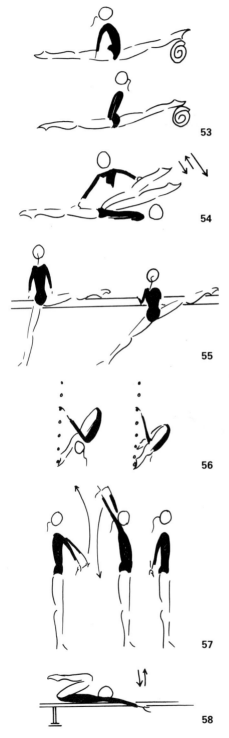

53

54

55

56

57

58

2 *The Floor*

Basic skills

The handstand

The handstand is basic to gymnastics, not only for floorwork but also for beam, bars and vault. It is therefore absolutely essential that it is performed correctly from the beginning and before any serious advance into other moves is made. Once this skill is learnt it is not to be pushed aside but to be practised as often as possible. A fault in the handstand can result in a fault in a more advanced skill.

The bunny jump to handstand

The gymnast prepares to take the weight on the hands by using the bunny jump. From squat position place the hands on the floor, shoulder width apart and pointing forwards (fig. 59). The hands should be just in front of the knees so that the arms are vertical. From this position the gymnast leans slightly forwards with the shoulders so that they are beyond the hands and pushes off the feet to lift the hips into the air. This practice is good for advanced gymnasts as well as beginners. It strengthens the body and gives the beginner more confidence in the inverted position. A common fault is that the gymnast places the hands too far away from the feet and then finds it difficult to get the hips above the hands.

59

At a more advanced level this practice can be changed slightly. From the same starting position the gymnast springs from the feet to lift the legs straight through a straddle position to handstand, then back to straddle and down (fig. 60). This can be repeated several times.

60

The handstand

Fig. 61 shows the correct handstand. Try to get a straight vertical line through the arms and up the back to the feet. The back *must* be straight. In any inverted support movement the shoulders must be lifted; the collar bone (clavicle) should be raised so that the shoulders come in close to the neck. It is most important that this movement and strength through the shoulders is obtained; at a later stage the gymnast must learn to drop and then extend her shoulders to achieve flight from the hands (study the back flip on page 40 and handspring vault on page 59).

To perform the handstand, a long step is taken through a fairly low position by the bending of the front leg. The arms are kept in line with the head. When the hands reach the floor the fingers meet the ground first so that contact is light, and this also helps to bring the shoulders over the fingertips and bring the body into balance. As the hands reach forward to the floor, the back leg (left leg in fig. 61) swings up to the vertical with a strong action. It is not until the hands have reached the floor that the front

61

A back handspring from cartwheel (Kanyo, Hungary).

A forward walk-over showing the tension and balance essential in artistic floorwork (Crabtree, GB).

leg (right leg in diagram) has finally straightened, pushed, and left the floor. It is then swung up to join the other leg and the final handstand position is shown.

From the first practice mistakes must be corrected. Check that the gymnast's hands are shoulder width apart. The fingers should be spread and the direction of the hands should be forward.

62

The handstand may be similar to the one shown in fig. 62, showing the back out of line with the shoulder creating an angle between the arms and the body. This may be caused by one or several of the following reasons:
1 The head may be lifted too high, creating a hollow in the back. The gymnast should be able to see no further forward than her fingertips.
2 The back may be too hollow due to lack of abdominal strength. The gymnast must improve her strength in this area in order that her back stays straight. Tension exercises are good for this (see page 26).
3 The shoulders may be stiff and not easily pressed back to form a straight line through the arms and back. The gymnast must, therefore, aim to loosen her shoulders. If they are very stiff she is going to have trouble with the backbend movements and must work very hard to correct this (see loosening exercises on page 27).

I often find that beginners kick up to a handstand and never reach a position of balance. In fig. 63 you can see that the gymnast is in a position where she is backwards over the 'heel' of the hand with her body arched to try and gain balance. This is caused by pushing the hands heavily into the floor with the 'heel' or the whole of the hand. This can be likened to the way in which one lands on the feet from a jump: the toes stretch for the floor and meet it first, followed by the rest of the foot, heel last. Also remember that when you are standing on your feet your weight is slightly over your toes.

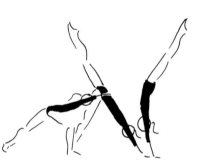

63

Balancing on the hands
Go back to the previous point, where the gymnast is in the position of standing on her feet. If she lets her weight go backwards over her heels she will lose balance and the only way to check this is to step back. If she tries leaning forward and lets all her weight rest on her toes, she will find that the action of her toes pressing on the floor maintains the balance. This principle must be applied to the handstand. Once the correct handstand position is achieved, with the weight slightly forwards and extension through the shoulders, balance should be easy, providing the gymnast has enough strength. Whilst in the position of balance the fingers should be moving by slight bending and stretching to correct any loss of balance. With the body strength there should be a pushing of the feet upwards, thus bringing about and maintaining a stretch through the shoulders and back. Not a great deal of strength in the arms is needed, as in most people there is a tendency for the arms to over extend at the elbow and therefore lock. If you have a gymnast whose arms never straighten, you can help to correct this by turning the hands out, thus bringing the front of the elbow

further forward and reducing the possibility of the elbows bending out to the side.

Overbalancing

If the gymnast is not prepared she may find that in overbalancing in the handstand she falls on to her back. She will not necessarily be skilled in the handstand bridge or roll at this stage. She must therefore be taught how to protect herself if she overbalances. One hand should be lifted off the floor and placed forwards and to the side. This brings the centre of gravity back and allows the gymnast to come out of the handstand as shown in fig. 64.

Coming down from handstand

One leg only is brought down to the ground, whilst the other is kept vertical for as long as possible (fig. 65). This means that the leading foot will land fairly close to the hands. As this leg lands there must be a good push from the hands to bring the body to a vertical position, with the arms kept by the ears and the stretch in the body maintained.

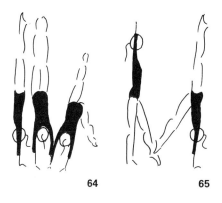

64   65

The forward roll

When learning this roll the gymnast must first learn how to stand up without using her hands.

This can be done with the gymnast sitting on the mat and clasping her knees as shown in fig. 66. She should then roll backwards and forwards twice and on the second roll forwards place the feet on the floor (keeping the legs bent), reach forwards with the hands, straighten the legs and stand up.

66

Next the gymnast can learn the complete roll (fig. 67). She should start about half a metre away from the edge of the mat. From squat position the gymnast must reach forwards to place her hands on to the mat and then roll forwards immediately to stand. The hands must be shoulder width apart and the gymnast must round her back as she goes into the roll. The legs should be straight. This cannot happen if the gymnast places her hands close to her feet. Having completed the first part of the roll the gymnast then bends her legs in order to stand up.

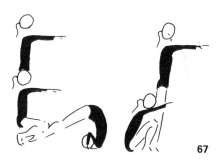

67

The backward roll

The backward roll (fig. 68) begins in the same position as the forward roll but with the heels to the edge of the mat. The head and arms are kept forward as the body is tipped back, so that the seat reaches the ground first, followed by the back. The hands are placed next to the back of the shoulders with the palms uppermost. As the body rolls backwards the hands are in contact with the floor. The body is curled tightly at this stage. Then there is a vigorous push with the hands, lifting the hips and quickly lifting the head. By the continuous movement of the roll the body is rotated on to the feet, with the gymnast pushing hard on the hands to bring her to an upright position.

68

31

A common fault in this basic bent leg roll is that the hands are placed on the floor from the beginning, before the body, thus touching the floor twice. This will often slow the momentum of the roll and thus break the continuity.

The cartwheel
The cartwheel (fig. 69) is started sideways to the direction of the move-ment. The action is similar to that of the handstand and the same leg is used to step. As in the handstand the stretch through the body must be maintained and the arms kept close to the ears. The leading leg must step to the side and bend on contact with the ground. The other leg swings into the air as the hands reach sideways to the ground, keeping in line with the body; the arms must keep close to the ears. When the first hand reaches the floor the swinging leg is well lifted and the other leg has straightened and pushed to rotate the body. The hands are placed as in the handstand, but do not touch the ground simultaneously. Notice that in the inverted position the legs are well apart. As the leading leg touches the ground there is a strong push from the last hand to bring the body upright and to keep the arms close to the ears. The final position shows a high leg lift.

69

The path of the cartwheel must always be a straight line. Gymnasts often take their hands behind the line of the feet. This means that the feet have to travel further as they not only have to go up and over the body but to one side as well. If the gymnast puts her hands well to the side of the straight line she may never pass through the vertical. Often a weak cartwheel indicates a weak handstand, so the gymnast should spend more time on the latter.

The one-handed cartwheel
Once the gymnast has mastered the cartwheel she can then learn the one-handed cartwheel. In fig. 70 the gymnast places her second hand (right in this case) on the ground. The free arm must swing to the side as

70

shown, as the swinging action aids rotation. The right hand is placed on the ground slightly nearer to the gymnast's last foot than in the two-handed cartwheel.

If support is needed, the coach stands behind the gymnast and places her left hand on the gymnast's left shoulder and the right hand on the left hip. This must be done when the gymnast is in the starting position and then the coach follows right through to the finish of the movement.

The cartwheel can also be done with the first hand only going on the ground (see fig. 83).

The handstand roll

The handstand forward roll (fig. 71) consists of two basic moves joined together. These must be performed as one, but the good technique of the original movement must still be maintained.

The handstand must be stretched and complete before the roll is begun. From the inverted stretch the arms are bent and then the head is tucked under so that it goes between the hands. The weight is taken on the shoulders and not on the head. You will notice at this point that the rest of the body is still vertical and well stretched. The rest of the body then rolls from the shoulders, until the weight is taken on the seat when the legs are bent, ready for the feet to touch the floor. The head and arms reach forward so that the gymnast may stand up.

71

In the learning stage gymnasts may find that they drop from the shoulders to the seat. To correct this the coach should hold the gymnast's ankles whilst she is performing the handstand, so that the legs and hips are kept vertical as the roll is begun. This ensures that the back is rounded.

The handstand bridge stand-up

The biggest problem that a gymnastics coach has is the number of gymnasts that she has at any one time to teach. If the coach has to stand in for every skill being learnt then obviously very little would be achieved. The gymnasts must, therefore, learn to stand in for each other in basic skills and the coach must break the skills down so that very little support is needed.

The handstand bridge can be broken down in such a way.

1 The gymnast must have a good handstand. She must have good control in the inverted position and be able to move the shoulders backwards. She may need to do this with a partner as it is difficult whilst trying to balance. The partner may also need to push the shoulders back on the first attempt. She can do this by turning the leg sideways and placing the side of the knee against the shoulder. She will need to put her foot between the gymnast's hands and will also need to keep the gymnast in a straight handstand so that she is stretched through the shoulders (see fig. 72). The gymnast should then learn to do this either balanced against a wall or with the partner just holding the feet.

2 The gymnast must have a reasonable bridge and therefore be fairly supple in the shoulders and back. It is difficult if she is very stiff but not impossible if she uses good technique. In the bridge position the gymnast needs to bend the legs and then push off them to straighten the legs in the air. This exercise requires strength and control, qualities that she will need in the final movement. Fig. 73b shows the shape that she should pass through before her feet touch the ground.

3 The standing up phase is difficult but this can be easily learnt with a partner. The two girls face one another as in fig. 74. The supporter holds firmly round the gymnast's back whilst she reaches backwards for the floor to come to bridge. She must keep her arms by her ears and stand with her feet slightly apart. Having come to bridge she must then stand up with the aid of the supporter. Notice how the supporter has placed her foot half-way between the gymnast's hands and feet; this will help her lift the gymnast easily. As the gymnast comes to stand she must take the hips forwards slightly. Again the arms must be kept by the ears. The gymnast needs to practise this exercise so that eventually she needs very little support.

Having mastered these three practices the gymnast can then try the whole movement with the aid of a partner. (If gymnasts learn to support one another in the simple skills when they are young they will under-stand gymnastics better and will probably become good coaches.)

The gymnast steps into handstand as advised before. Having reached the handstand she must then move the shoulders backwards. The sup-porter will put her near hand on the gymnast's shoulder and the far hand across the back. She may have to guide the gymnast here. As the legs move over to the ground they must be straight and controlled. Only at the last moment do the legs bend and move slightly apart. With the feet on the ground the gymnast then moves the hips forwards to stand.

The partner may have problems supporting her gymnast at first, but this does not matter. This way the gymnast will have to learn to do the

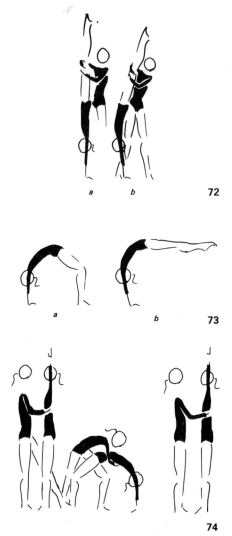

a b   72

a   b 73

74

skill quickly by herself; if an adult coach is constantly supporting then the gymnast often forgets or does not realize that she has to make an effort.

Notice how figs 75b and 75c correspond to the figs 72b and 73b. Control in shape in fig. 75c is vital.

b a c   d e   **75**

The forward walk-over

Many girls find this easier than the previous movement, but the hand-stand backbend must always be practised first to ensure good technique.

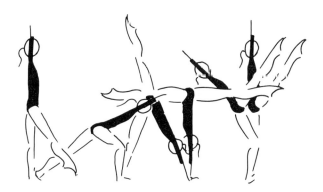

76

From fig. 76 you will see that the lead up to the handstand is the same as in all other cases, except that the legs do not come together but are kept in a complete split. It is more difficult to obtain a stretch in the body but the handstand must be achieved first with a stretch through the shoulders and back when the legs are in equal split. Before the first leg swings over to the ground the shoulders must move backwards. The second leg is kept high with the hips following. The final position is made with the arms held straight by the ears and the last leg held high.

If the head or the arms are brought forward before the movement is completed there will be a pike in the body. A pronounced pike may draw the gymnast backwards and cause her to fall.

The backward walk-over

Start with the leading leg pointed forward, arms up by the ears. Make sure that the back is straight. The arms move back first beyond the ears and then the head drops back as the back bends from the top. As the bend starts in the back so the leading leg lifts high from the ground. There is a slight forward movement of the hips at this stage. When the hands reach the floor and she is in handstand the gymnast should keep her back straight. The hips should then stay above the hands for as long as possible while the leading leg reaches the ground. Once the foot touches the floor

77

then the gymnast should lift from the ground keeping the arms by the ears (fig. 78).

The handspring

This agility is often underrated; girls find it particularly difficult. Practise it in three stages.

1 Start as for the handstand, taking a very long step forward, keeping arms by the ears. The legs swing and kick as usual but as soon as the hands touch the ground they must push away from the floor (fig. 79). The gymnast should never reach the handstand position and her legs will not necessarily be together. She should come down from this spring off the hands one foot after the other. This must be practised so that the gymnast does not 'give' or 'sag' in the middle of the back. If she does then she is not ready for this skill and should go back and do more work on body strength and tension exercises.

2 The gymnast should then practise the following (fig. 80) with the aid of the coach: kick to handstand as already described in the handstand section, the legs working very fast. The coach stands in front of the gymnast before she kicks to the handstand. As the gymnast kicks to handstand so the coach supports her round the waist with the hands or arms and allows the gymnast's legs to swing to the coach's shoulder. The coach must go in and meet the gymnast as she swings up. When the gymnast's hands touch the floor she pushes up. The coach aids but does not lift her, although upward flight should be achieved. The gymnast should have so much force that she tends to swing over the coach's shoulder.

78

79

80

3 Assuming that the two previous exercises are correct the gymnast then proceeds to the handspring (fig. 81). From the beginning the handspring should be trained with correct technique. Start from one step as before, straight into the handspring. The coach should lift under the shoulder

36

Above Reaching for the floor in a backward walk-over which the gymnast has extended further by standing on the ball of the supporting foot (Crabtree, GB).

Left A high leg lift coming out of a forward walk-over (Brooks, GB).

37

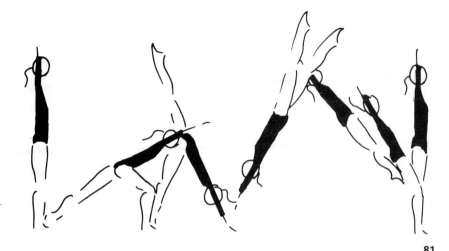

and on the lower back or bottom. Aid should be given by the coach in order to keep the shoulders back and to assist flight, but not to lift. The handspring must have lift off the hands and the legs must join together before touching the floor. As the first leg swings into the air it should go up as the hands push from the ground and the second leg should drive from the floor and aim to catch up with the first leg whilst it is still held high in the air. The joining of the legs, however, will normally be a short distance from the ground. During the flight off the floor the arms must remain by the ears. Common faults in the handspring are that the step in is too short or that the hands are dropped right down to the floor to create an angle in the shoulders. This increases the chance of the shoulders being too far forward over the hands on point of contact.

Preparation jump for handspring

If the gymnast is successful in the handspring from one step in, then she may learn the preparatory jump in. The gymnast should first start with two feet together and arms to her side but slightly back. From this position she should spring forwards and upwards co-ordinated with a swing of the arms upwards and forwards. From this two-footed take-off she should then land on one foot (if she steps left in handspring then she should land on the right leg), with the other leg kept to the back and then taken forward in a long step into what would be the handspring. The arms stay above the head. There should be a forward lean of the body. Once the timing of this is correct the gymnast can then take this into the handspring and then finally with one or two steps run in so that the two-footed jump comes from a short step, as seen in fig. 82. If the gymnast seems to get enough continuity and ease from her run (only two steps please) and good technique in the handspring without using the described preparatory jump, then do not bother to change it. Only do so if the gymnast is having problems.

82

38

The free cartwheel

This skill is quite simple for a fairly powerful and loose-limbed gymnast. Because of its simplicity the free cartwheel is often taught badly or not taught at all and the gymnast learns by trial and error. It can be practised in three stages.

1 The gymnast must learn to cartwheel starting from the front and then turn in to finish, landing one foot after the other and one in front of the other. Body tension and control is important. The hips must be square at the beginning of the cartwheel and at the finish.

2 Now the gymnast must do the same cartwheel but this time using one arm only, the same arm as leading leg. In fig. 83 the gymnast is using the left leg so the left hand goes to the ground. The free arm must be held to the side and not allowed to go across the body. The gymnast must maintain the same body shape and control that she had in the first practice.

3 Still following the same body pattern the gymnast now does the cartwheel with a drive off the front foot and off the hand (fig. 84). She must show lift in the second part of the cartwheel and still keep control.

83

84

85

Having perfected these three practices the coach must now come in and assist the gymnast through the whole movement. In fig. 85 the coach stands on the left side placing the right hand on the left hip and, as the gymnast turns over, places the left hand on the right hip. As the gymnast steps into the movement she swings the left arm downwards and backwards. The right arm remains to the side as it did in the previous practice. The swinging arm will move alongside the hips as in fig. 85. The gymnast lands as before bringing the swinging arm up by the head. In order to be successful the gymnast must co-ordinate the arm swing, the leg drive and the swing of the back leg. When the coach stands in she should feel the weight of the gymnast first on the right hand and then on the left hand. It is important that the coach realizes she must not lift the gymnast too much; the free cartwheel is not a high movement and too much lift would create the wrong action. Having supported the gymnast several times the

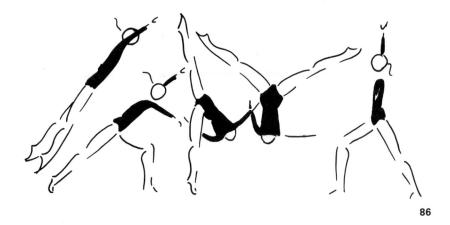

86

coach will know when the gymnast is doing most of the work herself. The coach can then support with the near hand only.

At this stage the gymnast can try the free cartwheel with a step and jump in and with only a little support. Finally the coach can stand back (fig. 86). The real test of whether the free cartwheel is good is for the gymnast to try it unaided just by stepping in as she did in the practices.

The correct arm swing is important: although the skill can be achieved without this it will never be good enough to transfer to the beam, so it is best to learn the correct way in the beginning.

The donkey kick

This activity is vital for the learning of the back flip, the round-off and the Tsukahara vault (see page 64).

Before attempting this movement (fig. 87) the gymnast does need a good handstand and strength in the shoulders.

From the handstand position the gymnast must allow the back to relax and the legs to bend. Notice that there is an angle between the arms and the chest. From this position the gymnast has to straighten out pushing away from the ground with the hands. She must pike down coming off the hands before the feet touch the floor. The gymnast must have relaxation in the body to initiate the movement. When jumping from the feet one has to bend the legs before pushing the body upwards; the same principle applies when jumping from the hands.

The gymnast must finish with the arms by the ears; the arms should be by the ears as the gymnast pushes from the ground and should stay there.

87

The back flip

Once this skill has been learnt it should always be preceded by a round-off or a cartwheel. It should, therefore, be taught with this in mind. It is not until much later that a gymnast needs to learn the skill of doing a standing back flip; she may need this for the beam or for part of a floorwork sequence, but this is not likely. There are three steps in learning the back flip.

1 The gymnast should start in a standing position with feet together and arms above her head. With the coach's aid she should then fold at the hips, still keeping her original form, so that she tends to fall back or may well do so if the coach is not there. The coach should support the gymnast across the back. From this position the gymnast must then open up the angle in the hips, so that the top half of the body is in line with the legs, leaning back at an angle (fig. 88). If the gymnast maintains her form in the preparation she is ready for the next stage.

2 The coach now stands behind the gymnast and puts one hand behind her neck and the other at the back of her waist, holding on to her leotard and top of her knickers. The gymnast does the same action again but as she tilts back she should bend the knees slightly and jump so that her weight is taken by the coach. Notice in fig. 89 how the back is slightly arched with the head and arms in line. Again, if the gymnast maintains form in the jump she is ready to progress to the next stage.

3 The coach should then kneel down at the side of the gymnast. Just for familiarity in going backwards the gymnast should then do one back bend to the ground and the coach helps to lift her feet off the ground together. The gymnast must then stand approximately 50 cms in front of the coach so that when supporting the coach has to reach towards the gymnast (fig. 90). The near hand is on the gymnast's stomach and the far hand on the back. The gymnast should then pike the body and jump backwards as before taking the head and arms back. As she begins the movement the coach should gently pull the gymnast back with the front hand. Once the gymnast has determined her path in flight this front hand (left in fig. 90) is then transferred to the thighs to help the legs over in the second phase. There is a short time when the gymnast is free in the air. At this stage the coach is supporting her with the second hand under the back (fig. 91). The hand should be flat on the back and forearm vertical with the elbow pointing to the ground. The coach must use her strength economically and not rely on forearm and bicep strength alone as perhaps a strong man can do.

When the gymnast's hands touch the floor she must push hard in order to snap the feet down close to the hands and lift the arms and body to the upright position. This is where the donkey kick action comes in.

The back flip off reuther board

The gymnast may experience some trouble in leaning backwards into the flip. This can be improved by standing on a sloping object such as a reuther board (fig. 92). The coach can stand in as before. It may help the gymnast if she thinks of driving from the heels. She should get the feeling of leaning back on the heels. When she actually drives from the floor the last part of the body to leave the floor will be the toes although she may

88

89

90

91

92

41

think she is coming from the heels. It is sometimes said that a gymnast is driving from her toes in a back flip which, in this instance, would be incorrect; what is meant is that the knees have been allowed to move forwards beyond the feet and the gymnast jumps upwards instead of backwards.

When the back flip is sufficiently practised and the gymnast needs only little assistance she is ready to do the cartwheel flip.

The cartwheel back flip
Start the cartwheel facing forwards (fig. 93) so that the step is the same as that for the handstand. The hands must be sideways as in a cartwheel. On the second phase the body must turn in to the hands and the first leg come in close to them; the second leg must then join the first leg so that they come down one after the other. The arms are lifted off the floor in a forward, upward and backward direction into the flip. The gymnast should practise the cartwheel first.

The advantage of the cartwheel flip is that the gymnast will find it easier to learn. It brings the body into the right position for the flip without having to have a good thrust off the hands. It is slower than the round-off flip so the gymnast can be more sure of herself and easier for the coach to stand in, particularly if the gymnast is a little uncertain. It is, however, a preparation and not a substitute for the round-off flip, so that as soon as it has been perfected the gymnast must move on to the round-off.

The round-off flip
The approach is as for the cartwheel flip, facing front. A long step is taken and the hands are placed on the floor one after the other, nearest hand first. A long reach is needed with the second arm so that there is no angle between the arm and body. The distance between the hands as they are

A perfectly performed split leap which can also be used on the beam (Hellmann, DDR).

Another example of a split leap, with back leg bent; variations on this provide good link movements in floor sequences (Hellmann, DDR).

a   b   c   d   e   f   g   h   i   j   k

on the floor is more than shoulder width apart, from half to the whole distance again. The hands should be straight or slightly turned as in fig. 94d and e. The push off the hands needs to be very powerful as the legs travel over the top of the body. When the legs are beyond the vertical they should be joined. Before the feet touch the floor the hands should have pushed from the floor so that for a certain time the body is free in the air (fig. 94f). The legs come down to the floor whilst the body is still rising and the arms swing forward and back into the back flip. Notice that in the drive from the feet the weight is well back beyond the heels going into the back flip. The learning of the donkey kick also assists in the last phase of the round-off.

The round-off two flips
Once the round-off flip is successful the gymnast needs to try the round-off two flips. She needs to create more power and by practising two flips after the round-off she can learn to increase her speed and drive.

The approach into the round-off is very important. The jump in should be as for the handspring so that the body is leaning forwards as the last step is made without losing the speed of the approach. This last step into the round-off must be low and fairly relaxed. The actual position of the hands on the floor may vary from gymnast to gymnast. The coach must look for a good drive off the hands to take the gymnast backwards with great speed and strength into the flip.

When the gymnast first learns a flip or round-off an essential coaching point is that the arms must be straight. As she becomes more confident this can be altered. In the donkey kick I talked about an angle between the arms and chest to initiate the drive from the hands. This drive can be increased by bending the arms slightly and driving out of this flexion. In the round-off I have already suggested that the hands should be turned inwards. This can be done in the back flip also, as it will restrict straining of the wrists (fig. 95).

It is important for the gymnast to understand that she does not need a long run into the round-off, a couple of steps will do and the power is increased by the speed of the legs as they drive from the floor in the

95

round-off. Speed is also increased by the drive from the hands (the donkey kick action) bringing the feet in fairly close to the hands in order to get the weight falling backwards into the flip. This must also happen at the end of the flip to increase the speed into the second flip. The second flip should be faster and more powerful than the first.

The gymnast must keep the head in line with the arms in the round-off and the back flips. It will tend to come out of line when the gymnast lands on her hands as the force will break the tension in the body, the break then being utilized to give more drive (see the donkey kick action in fig. 94i).

The back somersault

96

The back somersault (figs 96 and 97) is usually performed after a round off back flip but first of all the gymnast needs to do the skill from standing with assistance from the coach.

The coach should stand behind the gymnast holding round the waist with both hands. Starting with her arms held horizontal the gymnast then drops the arms, bends the legs slightly and swings the arms forwards and upwards as she jumps. The gymnast must not be hollow in the air but very slightly piked or dished as shown in fig. 96. The head needs to remain in normal body alignment. The coach should not lift the gymnast, just guide her. Having established that the gymnast has sufficient jumping power the coach can ask the gymnast to bend the legs at the top of the jump as shown in fig. 97. The gymnast must think of bringing the knees towards her chest and not taking the chest down to the knees. By pulling the knees up to the chest vigorously the hips should move forwards as seen in the diagram. If the gymnast cannot get the idea of this movement then the coach should try holding her at the top of both arms so that the hips are free to move. This is a little difficult as the coach has to relax the hold when the gymnast swings the arms downwards in the preparation.

97

When the gymnast can do the jump well she can move on to the complete somersault. The gymnast will either have to wear some track trousers or tie something firm round the waist for the coach to hold. The coach then holds on to the 'belt' and back of thigh as shown in fig. 98. As the gymnast jumps this time the coach lifts the hips so that the gymnast turns over in a somersault. The coach must keep hold of the gymnast with the hand on the waist. Rotation is set up by the lifting of the hips by the gymnast (helped by the coach) and by the swinging upwards of the arms which must stop immediately they reach the ears. The gymnast must try not to throw the head backwards. She may feel that this helps rotation but it will in fact open up the tuck position and therefore slow down rotation. The gymnast needs to become very familiar with the skill of turning over in the air. The quickest way to get in the number of repetitions required is to use the trampette (see page 50).

98

Having gained sufficient skill by using the trampette or with the coach the gymnast should then try the back somersault from the round-off flip.

99

The round-off back flip back somersault

Unlike the back flip the back somersault must go upwards for obvious
reasons. The back somersault is usually performed from the round-off
and the back flip. This will give the gymnast more power than just using
the round-off. It is not incorrect, though, to do the back somersault after
the round-off.

When coming out of the back flip in preparation for the back somersault
the gymnast must be in such a position that the jump goes upwards and
not backwards. This means that when coming out of the flip the gymnast
needs to reach backwards slightly with the feet so that as she extends the
body with the feet on the ground the gymnast is in fact leaning slightly
forwards (fig. 99). With angular momentum taking place by the time the
gymnast leaves the ground she is directed upwards.

First of all the gymnast needs to gain experience of going upwards out
of the back flip. The coach needs to stand in behind the gymnast as she
comes out of the flip, holding her just above the waist. The coach must
make sure that she gets to the gymnast early as her hands are leaving the
ground in the flip. This needs to be practised several times. An alternative
is for three or four crash mats to be piled up so that as the gymnast jumps
upwards any backward lean is saved by the mats.

Once this jump out of the flip has been mastered then the gymnast can
do all three skills together. The coach needs to follow the gymnast in the
round-off and the flip, putting the far hand under the back on the back flip
and keeping that hand in contact with the gymnast as she goes into the
back somersault. The near hand should be used to help rotate the gymnast by pushing at the hips. The coach should keep the far hand in contact
with the gymnast and, as the gymnast turns over, transfer the hand from
the hips to the abdomen as the gymnast comes down to the ground. The
early repetitions will be for familiarization only. Once the gymnast is
happy with the movement then you can try and improve the technique.

Opposite A double-twisting back
somersault showing height and
tension (Li Hui-Ping, China).

Below A dramatic pose suitable for the
conclusion of a floor exercise
(Shaposhnikova, USSR).

One of the most common faults is that the gymnast will throw her head backwards in the somersault. This only opens the body and therefore slows down rotation. Another fault is that the gymnast does not lift the arms from the back flip up into the extension before the tuck position but allows the arms to drop and clutch somewhere around the knees. This makes the somersault low.

It is not sufficient for the gymnast to turn over backwards in the air; she must turn over at her own head height and show form and control.

Another important aspect is, obviously, the landing. If the gymnast stays tucked for too long then she could over-rotate and fall backwards. Once the gymnast knows where she is in the air then she can try opening out sooner and reaching backwards with the feet. She should not reach downwards. When her feet actually touch the ground she should be inclined slightly forwards, again using the mechanical principle of angular momentum. The degree of lean in her landing will depend upon the height and rotation achieved; with very little height and rotation she will not be able to extend backwards with the feet as she is likely to fall forwards. The somersault should in fact contain three phases: the extension, the tuck and a second extension, and all these should take place in the air.

Training on the trampette

The trampette or mini trampoline has a strong rebound action. Using this action the gymnast is able to practise skills and repeat them many times with very little fatigue. This apparatus is therefore immensely useful in the rapid learning of complex skills. It is, however, very dangerous if used in the wrong way.

Safety points
1 The apparatus should always be fitted with safety pads; these are pads fixed over the springs and the frame.
2 The apparatus should be tested and checked. If parts are not assembled correctly the trampette could collapse. The coach should jump on the bed and check that it does not hit the floor. All springs should be in place.
3 The coach should teach the gymnasts how to use the trampette correctly and state the consequences if gymnasts play on the apparatus. Permanent disability has been caused from using this apparatus whilst playing.
4 The last and most important point is that, however carefully the coach follows the first three points, if the gymnasts are not physically prepared, are not spacially aware and lack body tension then they could be thrown out of control. This apparatus should not be used as an extra piece in a recreational class where inexperienced gymnasts might be tempted to use it without proper training.

Introducing the trampette

1 From standing on the trampette the gymnast swings the arms forwards and upwards jumping from the bed to land on the crash mat (fig. 100). The gymnast must show tension through the body when getting lift off the trampette and then show a well-controlled landing. If any part of her body is out of control after the second attempt then she needs more body preparation before going on the apparatus again.

2 Using the bench and trampette the gymnast can jump from the bench on to the spring bed to jump upwards, as in no. 1, to land on the mats. If successful then a few steps can be done along the bench on to the trampette.

3 The bench can continue to be used or the gymnasts can run along the floor and step on to the trampette as they would a reuther board. With increased confidence and skill a variety of jumps can be done: straight, tuck, star, straddle (see figs 168–71), and half and full turns round the long axis. The greatest degree of perfection and control is required.

100

If the bench is used as a run up platform it may be useful to place two benches side by side covered by a mat. This allows the gymnast to be more confident in her run.

Front tumbling

First method

Front somersaults can be done from a run. The gymnast must have experienced the front somersault before and should not learn it from the trampette, although it can be learnt from a reuther board.

Having achieved the front somersault off the trampette the gymnast can then try it piked. When this is good she could then try the piked front with half turn. This is very useful for the learning of the Yamashita vault (fig. 125) with half turn. The gymnast makes the turn from the pike by turning as she extends the body.

The gymnast can learn to step out of the front somersault using the trampette in this way. When doing the front somersault to land only, two crash mats are needed, placed end to end with a mattress on top to cover up the join and to make the surface firmer. To join skills together three or four crash mats need to be placed end to end and two layers of long mattresses placed on top.

Coming out of the front somersault the gymnast should come down one foot after the other stepping out into a round-off flip. This could then be extended into round-off flip back somersault. This type of activity can also be done off a reuther board.

Second method

Effort required in the run can be eliminated by the following method which is also useful if space is limited.

Place the box next to the trampette as in fig. 101. The gymnast then drops from the box on to the trampette. As she drops she swings the arms

101

downwards and backwards ready to swing them forwards and upwards in the jump off the bed. Once acquainted with the set-up the gymnast can lead up to the front somersault and then the piked front walk-out as described previously. The mats should be arranged as before.

Care must be taken by the coach that the mats do not slip. They will need to be checked constantly.

Back tumbling

First method

Apparatus is arranged as in fig. 102.

The gymnast should stand with her hands gripping either side of the box top. With one bounce she jumps to handstand. From the handstand she then pikes down on to the bed and jumps backwards on to the mats. Her arms should stay by her ears as she lifts the hands off the box.

After several repetitions the gymnast can then back somersault from the jump on to the crash mat (fig. 103). It is advisable for the coach to stand in for the first attempts. The back somersault should be done from a one bounce introduction. If two or three bounces are encouraged then this extends to four or five and so on. This leads to tiredness for both coach

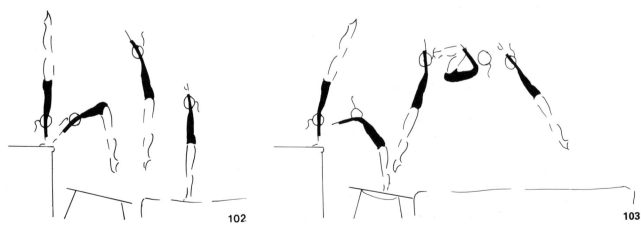

102

103

104

and gymnast and indecision which can lead to accidents. To increase the amount of lift to jump into handstand the gymnast could step in on to the trampette coming on to two feet and then bouncing to handstand.

When the technique is good then the gymnast could try the straight back somersault. The gymnast bounces on the trampette as before and lifts the arms off the box top. She must think of lifting the feet upwards once the thrust has been made. When the gymnast is approximately horizontal the body should have caught up with the arms which should be against the thighs. When supporting the straight back somersault the coach will need to give assistance under the thighs as well as the middle of the back.

To learn a series of tumbling skills the crash mats and mattresses can be arranged to form a platform as described on page 49. For improving the landing as well as the difficulty value at the end of the back somersault the gymnast can then try a back flip. Another back flip and back somersault could be added to this.

Second method

This method is probably the most useful. The apparatus should be arranged as shown in fig. 104, with two benches placed side by side to give a safe run-up and with the trampette in the flat position. A mat should be placed over the benches.

First, the gymnast needs to mark out her approach. Facing the trampette and standing on the benches she should round-off, placing her hands on the bench and feet on the trampette bed. Having established where her hands should be placed this can then be marked on the surface with some chalk. The feet must always land in the centre of the trampette bed. The first skill should be the round-off to jump on to the landing surface. The gymnast can then perform the round-off into the back somersault.

When the gymnasts have got used to this piece of apparatus they will always want to do trampette tumbling. The coach must remember that this is only a training method and cannot be used in competition. After working on the trampette the gymnasts need to go back to the floor.

3 The Vault

Many years ago vaulting was rather a static activity, where the gymnast showed some shape on top of the horse. To arrive in handstand and to be able to balance for a fraction of a second before overswinging or squatting between the hands was quite fantastic. Originally vaulting was performed with pommels on the horse, which was rather tricky if you missed one. As vaulting developed, more emphasis was placed on the first flight and the distance from the board to the horse.

The coming of male gymnasts Yamashita and Tsukahara from Japan changed all this. The vaults that they invented concentrated on second flight, which needed to be higher than the first. It was found that with a long first flight the gymnast had more time to rotate, thus coming on to the horse at a high angle. The only way out of this was to have a low flight off or even drop out of it (see fig. 105). By increasing the speed and bringing the board in closer it was found that the gymnast could strike the horse at a lower angle and get a higher second flight, an essential for a one-and-a-half back somersault off (the Tsukahara vault).

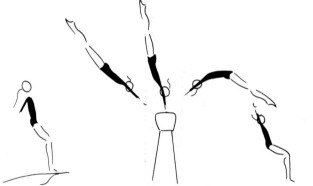

105

For vaulting, as for tumbling, the legs must be strong and the gymnast must be able to run fast. Statistics show that medal winners on vault at Olympic and World Championships are the fastest runners. It is very important when selecting young gymnasts that a close look is taken at their ability to run and jump, without bias towards suppleness and basic skill ability. Often very supple girls are weak when it comes to running and jumping; they will not make very good gymnasts.

Even though running and jumping can be considered the first requirements for vault it is often considered best to teach your gymnast first how to land, essential for safety. The teaching of the basic vault will be done in reverse order; the landing, shape on the horse and second flight, take-off and first flight and finally the run.

The basic vault

The landing

In order to have a good landing the gymnast must have a good jump. She must be stretched in the air before contact with the floor is made. This can be practised on the floor or off a bench or a box.

Any jump is aided by the upward swing of the arms as the gymnast thrusts from the ground, straightening the legs. The preparation bend should be only slight as shown in fig. 106, bending at the ankles, knees and hips. With the forward and upward swing of the arms and the simultaneous straightening of the joints mentioned the thrust is created. This means that the legs and ankles should be stretched when they leave the floor.

106

Many beginners hollow the body when they jump, throwing the arms, head and legs backward. They do not get maximum drive from the ground if they do this. If anything the body should be slightly piked or dished to get maximum drive.

Now to the landing from the vault: as with any landing the first part of the body to touch the floor should be the bottom of the toes. They then flex and the ball of the foot touches and finally the heel. As the heel touches so the ankle, knee and hips bend. Even though the body 'relaxes' on contact to make the landing as smooth as possible there must be a certain amount of tension in the body so that the gymnast does not sink too low. Using only a shallow bend the gymnast must then be ready to stand up straight again. In the first dismounts from vault or any other piece of apparatus the gymnast should land with the heels together and the toes turned out slightly. It is not a good idea to land with the feet straight and together. This makes the landing base very small.

In more advanced vaults, especially those with a twist in the second flight, it is safer to land with the feet slightly apart and use a greater knee bend. As the gymnast straightens the body she should draw the feet together.

The landing is absolutely vital in all apparatus work but more particularly on the vault. However good the vault, if the gymnast falls forwards or sits backwards or even hops forwards, it has been spoilt. Much attention should be paid to the landing. The gymnast should learn to adjust the position of her body to correct any overbalancing. Two gymnasts working together can do this. One should stand as shown in fig. 107, and the other pushes her gently to take her off balance. By lowering or lifting the hips she can maintain balance (as long as she is not grossly overbalanced). The pushing of her toes or heels into the floor is also important.

As the gymnast comes in to land the arms are above the head. This is where they should stay until the gymnast straightens the body. Then they can come to the gymnast's side.

To counteract the forward momentum the gymnast needs to reach

107

forwards with the feet before landing. From a static jump the forward momentum will not be great but from a handspring vault it will be greater and the gymnast will have to reach further forwards.

Shape on the horse and second flight
It is often the squat or straddle vault that the gymnast learns to perform first. For the purpose of this preliminary training it is best to combine the two vaults: for this stage I suggest you use the straddle and for the next, the squat. The cat spring action, bringing the legs into squat position, can be practised on the floor first.

The box is placed lengthways (the box is very useful for vault practices and for this particular one better than using the horse lengthways).

From a squat position on the end of the box the gymnast swings the arms forwards and upwards reaching for the end of the box. As she does this she thrusts from her legs, stretching the body as the hands come into contact with the end of the box. The gymnast then parts the legs to straddle, pushing off the hands to stand on the mat. It is advisable for the coach to stand in for the first attempts (fig. 108). She should stand at the end of the box facing the gymnast. As she reaches forwards with the arms the coach should hold her at the top of the arms. Although the coach starts to support the gymnast standing close to the box, as the gymnast thrusts from the hands and moves forwards the coach must move back to give the gymnast room to move. Still holding the gymnast by the arms she should lift the gymnast's arms upwards as she thrusts from the end of the box.

108

For early attempts or for small gymnasts the movement can be started half-way along the box. As the gymnast becomes more confident she should move backwards.

At a later stage the practice on the box can be used to help increase push-off and second flight for the straddle and for the squat vault. When working for improved quality the gymnast must push hard off the hands, try to straighten the body before landing and aim to get lift off the box.

Left A first flight for the handspring vault showing the correct angle between chest and arms (Leighton, GB).

Below left Good body tension is shown in this second flight in the handspring full twist vault (Leighton, GB).

Below The pike in the second flight in the Yamashita vault must be less than ninety degrees, as shown (Lennox, GB).

Take-off and first flight

This phase of the vault will need the most preparation. I have therefore given several practices.

1 First the gymnast must practise the jump and the arm swing. This is very similar to the practice that was done for landing (fig. 106). On the jump the gymnast should tighten up the muscles throughout the body so that the gymnast is in a state of tension. She should not jump allowing the legs to be straight without any muscle tone. The arms should not be swung behind the ears but should stay just in front. Landing should be on two feet as for landing in vaulting.

2 The gymnast must practise the same jump but with a step before. This can be taught to a large group of gymnasts together. As the gymnast steps forwards she swings the arms behind the body. She then joins the second foot to the first and, bending the knees as in fig. 109c, is ready to jump. The jump is as before. This same practice can then be done with a few running steps.

3 Arrange a bench, board and crash mat as shown in fig. 110. The gymnast runs along the bench taking off one foot at the end and landing on the board on two feet. The gymnast should not run so fast that she cannot control the jump. Using a bench for the run-up does limit the amount of speed that can be gained. It is also very good in a class in that everyone can see the complete working area and the extent of the run-up.

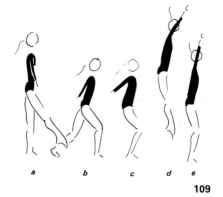

109

| a | b | c | d | e |

110

4 Flight on to the horse, whether it is for a squat or a handspring, is not just vertical but passes through the horizontal and rotates (particularly for the handspring).

Using the same apparatus as before the gymnast jumps from the board and swings the arms forwards to forward roll on the crash mat (fig. 111). As the gymnast becomes more confident greater height and stretch can be made in the air.

5 Still using the bench and reuther board, a box can now be introduced. On first attempts it is better to turn the box lengthways (fig. 112). If the gymnast does fall forwards after the squat she only falls on to the box. In the squat the hands are placed shoulder width apart and go to the end of

111

the box. The board needs to be at least half a metre away from the horse for the gymnast to achieve anything like a good first flight. If the gymnasts are small then obviously the box can be lowered.

Notice in fig. 112b how the gymnast is leaning back as she strikes the board; the hips are behind the knees with the shins vertical. If the gymnast lands on the board as shown in fig. 113 then there will be too much rotation forwards and she is likely to fall forwards instead of squatting on to the box.

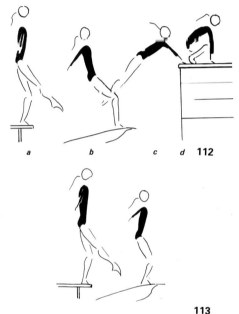

a   b   c   d   112

The run
When using a bench for the run-up as shown in previous practices the length and the speed of the run is limited. The coach should concentrate on teaching the gymnasts how to run in a relaxed manner which is efficient and can be speeded up with increased effort on the part of the gymnast. As the gymnast improves so the speed of the run will need to improve. For the squat vault, as against the squat on, the run will need to be faster and longer.

A good way for gymnasts to improve the power in their runs and also the use of their arms is that shown in fig. 114. The gymnast on the left runs forwards whilst the one on the right provides some resistance, just enough to allow the gymnast to run but with difficulty. The one providing the resistance will also have to run, but backwards.

113

The squat vault
Often the first complete vault to be attempted by any gymnast is the squat. A horse or a box can be used but it should be widthways as with all women's vaulting. The height required for the apparatus in international and most national competitions is 120 cms. At regional competitions the height may be lower. In training it is better that the coach puts the horse at a height that is suited to the gymnasts.

The length of run for a squat vault will vary from approximately seven metres to fifteen metres. It should not be so long that the gymnast tires by the time she reaches the board, but it must be long enough for the gymnast to have obtained a good speed. The board will need to be 50 to 100 cms away from the horse.

114

If the gymnast is too upright as she comes on to the board then it may be that the length of her last step on to the board, the hurdle step, is too short. Check the distance of the last step. It may be anything from 100 to 150 cms. If the take-off is at the edge of the board it is likely that the gymnast is not very powerful and does not have a fast run.

As soon as the gymnast is able to perform a squat vault (fig. 115) with good first flight and second she needs to measure the length of her run and the distance of the board from the horse. As the gymnast becomes more powerful the length of her run will increase. She may be doing eleven steps in her run, but due to increased strength she covers more ground with the same eleven steps. If the board distance is changed then the starting point for the run must be changed to keep the length of the run constant.

a   b   c   d   e   f   115

As the gymnast reaches for the horse with her hands the shoulders should be behind the hands as shown in fig. 115b. By the time the gymnast actually squats over the horse the hands should be off the horse and moving upwards having pushed from the horse. The body must extend before landing. Notice the reaching forwards of the feet ready for landing in fig. 115e.

For the gymnast to reach the horizontal position in first flight she needs speed in her run. Her jump off the board must be powerful and she must have good control and tension throughout her body. If the body is piked in first flight it may simply mean that the gymnast is weak, particularly in the seat muscles (gluteals). With more body conditioning, providing that the technique and understanding of the vault is good, the vault should improve; a weak gymnast will perform a weak vault.

One of the common faults in the squat vault is that the shoulders are over the hands as they contact the horse (the strike). This could mean that the board is too close to the horse and the gymnast does not have room to stretch or simply that the gymnast is not swinging her arms past the right angle with her chest.

Ideally, as with most other vaults, the length and height of the second flight should be greater than the first. This will not be so if the gymnast goes well above horizontal on the first flight; she will probably fall forwards landing on knees and then hands.

It is advisable to stand in for gymnasts at the squat vault stage, particularly for those with less experience. The coach should stand on the side of the horse furthest away from the board (the second side) and support the gymnast with both hands on the top of her near arm. When the gymnast is moving fast the coach must make sure that she is ready to move forwards with the gymnast and not wrench her arm off by staying by the horse. The coach must also be ready to move her hands up as the gymnast lifts her arms.

The straddle vault

This vault is very similar to the squat vault, the only difference being that the gymnast straddles her legs as she passes over the horse. The gymnast must join her legs before landing. The coach stands in as for the cat spring straddled off the box (see fig. 108).

Advanced vaults

The handspring vault

This is the first of the inverted vaults. With these vaults the gymnast completes a somersault with the hands touching the horse before half of the somersault has been completed. In some ways this vault is less complicated than the squat vault. I think that a group of well-prepared young gymnasts can effectively ignore the squat vault and go straight on to the handspring, using the following progressions.

1 Use a box top and a crash mat. The gymnast should kick up to handstand and then fall flat on to her back (fig. 116). The gymnast must have good body tension so that she touches the mat as one, not with heels or bottom first.

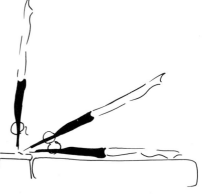

116

2 Now introduce the reuther board. For first attempts the coach will need to stand in or in this case sit in. The coach sits astride the box and supports the gymnast with the near hand on the stomach and the far hand on the back. With a short run the gymnast then jumps from the reuther board on to her hands on the box top and springs off, flat on to her back on the crash mat (fig. 117).

The gymnast should be straight as she hits the box top. Notice how the gymnast is at an angle of approximately 55 degrees as she strikes the box. Providing she is running fast, this angle should give her enough rotation to come off the box and land on her back. If, however, the gymnast does not have a fast run then she will need to come on to the box top at a slightly higher angle. You may find the weak gymnast pikes up to the handspring.

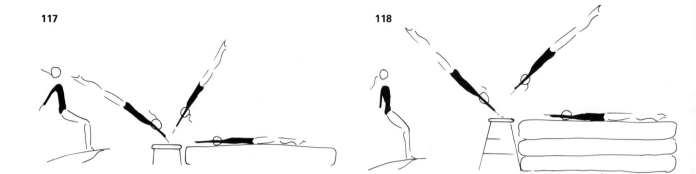

To run fast and come on to the box at about 55 degrees is the ideal but if your gymnast is not prepared sufficiently then there is no way she will be able to do this.

If the gymnast performs the handspring well after several practices then there is no need to stand in.

3 More layers can be added to the box (fig. 118) and the level of crash mats built up so that the gymnast still lands flat on the back.

4 Once the gymnast is performing well it is not advisable to continue with the landing on the back. She must now learn to continue the rotation and land on her feet. Set up two pieces of vaulting apparatus in a T-shape (fig. 119). The distance of the gap, if there needs to be one, will depend upon the size of the gymnasts. From the long box the gymnast steps into a handspring. Get the gymnast to swing the arms forwards and upwards as she steps forward, as she would in the arm swing in first flight. The legs should join past the vertical. The gymnast must then keep the body straight, allowing the rotation created to take her to her feet. On first attempts the gymnast will probably hollow so it helps if the coach stands in to try and correct this. The coach's near hand must go on to the gymnast's shoulder supporting her between the thumb and fingers and the far hand goes on to the gymnast's bottom. Both handholds are very

119

important. The first must grip the shoulder so that when the gymnast lands the coach still has her shoulder and is able to stop over-rotation; the second hand stops the gymnast hollowing the body. Many coaches make the mistake of placing the second hand at the back of the waist. If the gymnast is weak she invariably hollows and over-rotates on to the knees or forwards on to the hands, particularly if the coach is not gripping her tightly by the top of the arm.

5 Now it is time for the final vault. The horse does not need to be at 120 cms, especially if the gymnasts are small and young. It is better to learn a good technique and flight pattern on a low horse than a bad technique on a high horse. As the gymnast grows so the apparatus can grow, and her technique can remain constant.

The length of her run and distance of the board can be the same as it was for practice no. 3. The coach can stand in on the second side as she did for the previous practice. Some coaches stand in on the first side, between the board and the horse. The gymnast very soon gets used to this. There are dangers, however: the coach could lift the gymnast too high on the first flight and cause over-rotation, or, when the coach does not stand in, the gymnast is often petrified.

Improving the handspring vault

It is well worth spending time on the handspring as it leads in to other more difficult vaults: the Yamashita, the handspring with full or one and a half twist, and the handspring front somersault.

When the gymnast first learns this vault she must keep the body straight all the time and get her thrust off the top of the horse by the push through the shoulders and hands. She must not bend the arms. There are some things that will happen automatically that she may not be aware of, providing she keeps good body tension and uses her strength in the push off. Because the body that hits the top of the horse is human and not a solid stick then some collapsing is bound to occur. On impact the gymnast will give in the shoulders and there will be a slight relaxation of the chest or thorax. A good gymnast will push out of this and extend the body once more as she leaves the horse. If she has good strength and understands the vault sufficiently, she can develop this natural action.

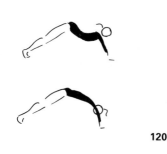

120

First of all get the gymnast to stand on all fours as in fig. 120. Keeping the arms still, she should drop her chest and then lift it upwards so that first she makes an angle between the arm and chest and then she extends the angle to a near straight line. This practice can also be done with the aid of the coach or partner (fig. 121). Hold the gymnast's thighs and get her to perform the same two actions. Start with the shoulders back from the hands so that the gymnast is placed near the angle that she would be at strike on the horse. It may be necessary to assist the gymnast under the chest with one hand as this position is very difficult for the gymnast to hold. Notice that in both practices the head is up and then down. The head should not move independently but as an extension of the spine.

121

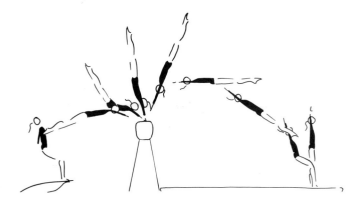

122

If you are satisfied that the gymnast understands the action and is strong enough to cope then get her to try this action in the handspring vault (fig. 122). As the gymnast takes off from the board she must be 'sucked in' as always but as the heels lift she can then drop the chest so that she strikes the horse in a slightly hollow position. This hollow will be taken further on impact with the horse and then the gymnast has to push out of the hollow rapidly, extending the whole body into second flight. If the gymnast is weak then on strike she will collapse too much and hurt her back and certainly will not have the strength to extend out. Notice again how the gymnast's head position has changed, up on the first flight and in between the arms on second flight. Many beginners see the better gymnasts doing this and copy the head action without understanding that it comes from the spine; they therefore lack height in second flight.

Using this action the gymnast is making more angles in the body to extend from the hands than she would for a jump from the feet (fig. 123).

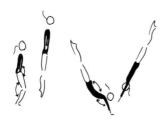

123

The Yamashita vault

If the gymnast has learnt the dropped chest action in the handspring then she is going to get on well with the Yamashita. This vault has a pike in the second flight before opening out to land.

1 The gymnast must learn to bring the chest to the legs to create the pike and not the legs to the chest. The coach can hold the gymnast as shown in fig. 124 and then the gymnast folds rapidly up to the legs.

2 The second flight needs to be practised first either with a trampoline (see fig. 133), or with a T-shaped horse (see fig. 119). Once the gymnast's hands have touched the apparatus she starts to lift the chest to the legs. The pike must be tight (fig. 125e). After the pike the gymnast must extend the body well before landing. The coach can stand in just as she did for the handspring vault, one hand on the shoulder and the other supporting under the seat.

124

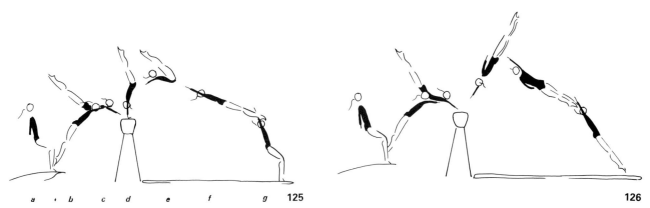

a   b   c   d   e   f   g   **125**　　　　　　　　　　　　**126**

Because the gymnast is piked for some of the second flight the rotation is speeded up. If the gymnast came on at the same angle as for the handspring vault the gymnast would probably over-rotate. She can, therefore, come on at a slightly lower angle in first flight. This could be something between 40 to 55 degrees. The angle will depend upon speed and technique of the gymnast. First flight will be lower if the board is brought in slightly. The distance to be moved will have to be found by trial and error. It could be as much as 25 cms. The gymnast must think of swinging the hands to the horse as quickly as possible to get the low flight on.

As soon as the gymnast has touched the top of the horse (fig. 125d) she should start piking, lifting the chest to the legs. Using the drop chest in first flight the gymnast is able to use the action of the hollow to help her to lift into the pike. Notice that the gymnast does not pass through a straight handstand on top of the horse. The pike should be no more than 90 degrees, less is better. Whilst the back is still nearly horizontal the gymnast must open the pike to extend. A good Yamashita is often recognized by the height and angle of the extension after the pike.

The handspring full twist vault
The gymnast can learn this vault (fig. 126) by using either the box top, horse and crash mats or a trampoline and crash mats. She can do many repetitions of the handspring full twist landing on the back on the crash mat. The coach will not need to support the gymnast.

Before she practises the twist she must learn the correct arm action. To twist to the left, the gymnast brings the right arm down to the side by moving it forwards and downwards. She should practise this several times, push from the horse, bring right arm down and land on the back. All the time the gymnast does this she should keep the body absolutely straight. Any bend in the body will slow down the twist.

When satisfied that the arm pattern is established the gymnast can then turn the head to the left as the arm is brought downwards and turn to the

left. First attempts may only take the gymnast half-way or three-quarters round. If the gymnast starts to lose the correct technique then she must go back to just the handspring, bringing the arm down.

When the twist is established it can be tried on the T-shaped apparatus or the trampoline. Finally the whole vault can be attempted on the horse.

The twist should be seen to begin after the gymnast has left the horse and completed before she lands.

The Tsukahara vault

This vault is a turn on to the horse in first flight followed by a one and a half back somersault off. The turn on to the horse can be anything between a quarter to a half turn. This vault can be dangerous if not given enough preparation. There are many practices that can be used before attempting the final skill. The gymnast must be both a competent vaulter and well prepared before attempting this vault.

1 Using the reuther board, box top and crash mat (see fig. 127), the gymnast has a short run-up, turning in first flight to push off the hands and land on her front on the crash mat. The gymnast should try and come on to the box top low. She should practise this until she is confident about the turn.

2 Using the box top and crash mat the gymnast should kick to handstand on the box and then donkey kick down to the feet. After several attempts at this she should then go right on to the back without the feet touching the mat (fig. 128). The legs are bent in the handstand and the chest is slightly dropped creating an angle between the chest and arms. Using the kick of the legs and the extension through the shoulders and wrists the gymnast must then get a powerful push off. The arms stay by the ears.

3 The previous two practices are now joined together. The gymnast turns on to the box top and then pushes off to come on to the back. The first flight must be fairly low and the gymnast must keep the legs straight and together until she pushes off the box and begins to tuck.

Opposite The Tsukahara vault (piked) in nine stages, from top left to bottom right (Comaneci, Romania).

4 Using a box or horse the gymnast should practise a standing back somersault to land on the floor.

5 Either a T-shape set-up or a sloping trampoline can be used now. From the approach the gymnast turns on to the horse completing the half turn as she pushes off to land facing the horse on her feet, as in a round-off (fig. 129). She must get good lift in second flight. She should land on two or three crash mats. After several attempts she should allow the body to rotate slightly more so that she falls backwards on to the mat.

The coach should practise standing in for the gymnast as the stand-in technique now will be the same as for the Tsukahara. Standing at the side of the horse the coach will put the nearest hand to the horse on the gymnast's tummy. The far hand then goes on the middle of her back.

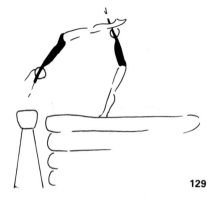

129

6 At least three crash mats should be used so that the landing surface is nearly as high as the take-off surface. Again either the T-shape or the trampoline can be used.

The gymnast comes into the first flight and then pushes off for the second, tucking the body tight after the push (fig. 130). There should be one or two coaches supporting. As the gymnast comes on to the horse the coach's near hand goes into the tummy; this hand helps keep the gymnast high and is also a point round which she can rotate. The second hand will now go further down the back across the back of the hips. This hand must be pushed away from the horse and downwards to help rotate the gymnast in the somersault. Many repetitions should be done of this practice. If the gymnast fails to push off then she must go back to the previous practice. If there were two coaches one coach can now be taken away. When greater competence is achieved a crash mat can be taken away.

130

7 Using the horse on its own with the reuther board and crash mats, much practice must be spent on turning on to the horse in first flight and pushing off to land facing the horse (fig. 131). When both coach and gymnast are satisfied the whole Tsukahara vault can be attempted. Again the crash mats should be built up, with three at least. The coach or coaches will stand in as before. Finally, the crash mats can be removed one by one.

a   b   c   d   e   f   g

131

Improving the Tsukahara vault

The flight on should be angled between 35 and 45 degrees from the horizontal. The board needs to be fairly close to the horse so that the low first flight is achieved. The turn can be a quarter, three-eighths or a half. Contact with the horse will invariably be one hand slightly after the other. The position of the hands is not important for the judges and may in fact have the fingers slightly down the side of the horse. With the gymnast coming on at such a low angle there would be tremendous strain on the wrists if the hands were directly on top of the horse. It is not necessary to coach the gymnast in hand placement but she need not think that hands slightly down the front of the horse is incorrect.

The gymnast should try and push off the horse at about 90 degrees. At this point the legs will have started to bend (fig. 131d). It is vital for the success of the Tsukahara that the second flight is high; the gymnast needs height to complete the one and a half somersault. As the hands leave the horse they should be brought into the body to complete the tuck position.

The tighter the tuck position the faster the gymnast will rotate. She should aim to have completed the rotations by the time she is level with the horse. Extension of the body should start here (fig. 131f).

The gymnast will need to extend the feet backwards slightly to stop over-rotation on landing. It is advisable to land with the feet slightly apart, using a deep knee bend to absorb the shock on landing.

Vault training

A training session on the bars of forty-five minutes is only just adequate for six gymnasts on one set of bars. The same time for the same gymnasts on vault could be very exhausting if they spent all their time running and vaulting. In the training of vaulting several things need to be considered.

1 The coach must consider the gymnasts' condition at the end of the session. If they work hard on vault alone they are probably not going to be fit to work another piece of apparatus following this or even the next day.

2 If the gymnasts do the same activity all the time they will get bored and probably not learn a great deal.

3 A single vault is over in a matter of seconds. This does not mean that less time need be spent on this activity. A gymnast can still score ten marks on vault, the same as for any other piece of apparatus.

4 One of the most common injuries in top British gymnasts is that they get shin soreness. This is often caused by a lot of vaulting, so training that concentrates on second flight only is going to help relieve this problem. The soreness is caused by continual running, often on cold hard gym floors. A vault run-up, a strip of matting that provides some padding but is not too soft, will help to cushion the floor.

Taking these things into consideration the coach must give the gymnasts plenty of variety and different situations in order to achieve the desired result.

132

Apparatus for vault practice

1 In the early stages of a vault it may help the gymnasts to gain the correct technique if they can get more lift on to the horse. This can be done by using two reuther boards as shown in fig. 132. This should not be used for too long.

2 A box top can be used to introduce twisting vaults (fig. 117).

3 A T-shape can be set up using a box and a horse. This is very useful for the second phase of the vault.

4 A trampoline can be used. This is arranged as shown in fig. 133. The gymnast steps forwards to bounce on the trampoline bed on two feet and then jumps forwards swinging the arms forwards as she would in first flight in vault. As in the previous practice this is good for second flight practice.

133

5 Three or four crash mats can be piled on top of one another. A reuther board is then placed in front and the gymnast vaults on to the crash mats. This is especially useful for working on first flight and for vaults that involve a twist in first flight.

6 If you are lucky enough to have a pit then vaulting can be done into this. It is also useful to use two reuther boards on top of one another in front of the pit and use these as a take-off platform for the hands. The gymnast can round-off on to the boards taking off one foot after the other and then Tsukahara into the pit. This must be done after suitable preparation practices. Other vaults could also be practised in a similar manner. The advantages of this method are that the gymnast gets a certain amount of lift off the hands from the boards and that it is safe, the gymnast being so close to the landing surface.

4 The Beam

Since the first edition of this book in 1972 rapid progress on the beam has been made. Back flips on the beam are so common that nobody talks about them any more; free walk-overs and somersaults are also increasing in number. The International Committee therefore decided that the gymnast's welfare must be more carefully considered. It was with this in mind that the padded beam was introduced. The beam is still 500 cms long, 16 cms deep and 10 cms wide but it is now surrounded by a padded synthetic leather case. The time of the beam exercise is one minute fifteen seconds to one minute thirty-five seconds.

Although there are four pieces of apparatus in the Olympic programme, two of them are so alike that skills for one can be transferred to the second. If a coach has to teach a skill on the beam it usually means that it has not been taught on the floor. Only mounts and dismounts are peculiar to beam and even these should be achieved on the floor in some way before transferring them to apparatus.

Beam skills must therefore only ever be transferred to the beam and not taught on it. This can be made more gentle by the introduction of other apparatus.

Preparation sequence for beam skills

1 The floor.
2 A line on the floor.
3 The broad side of a wooden bench (fig. 134a). Carpet can be wrapped round the bench and tacked to the underside.
4 A floor beam. This can be made very simply and cheaply. It does not have to be five metres long and can be 10 cms × 10 cms. It can be mounted on low feet at either end, or left as it is on the floor (fig. 134b). Again this can be covered with carpet.
5 A low beam.
6 A high beam (fig. 134c).

Mounts and dismounts need not be transferred to the beam straight away; vaulting boxes can be used for cartwheel and handstand dismounts and for free dismounts. They can also be used for many mounts. Sometimes in a school hall, which may be your gymnastic centre, there is a stage. This is ideal for beam mounts and dismounts.

Warm-up

The warm-up on the beam is not a wholly physical warm-up; it should also be a mental one, a relaxation of the nerves, so that more daring moves can follow. These conflicting ideas make the beam a very difficult piece of

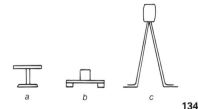

a   b   c   **134**

apparatus; it is probably the piece that needs the most time for adjustment. The warm-up must be a build-up, as in all other cases. The gymnast can get on to the beam by any method.

She must begin by walking along the beam, stretching each foot before it comes into contact with it. She must have good posture and poise; the head must be held up and she must not look down at the beam. At the end of the beam she should rise up on her toes, her weight evenly placed on both feet, and pivot so as to turn and continue back along the beam again. This method of turning can be used all the time in the warm-up and can in itself be a form of training. As the weight is taken on the balls of the feet the leg and seat muscles must tighten up more to maintain her balance.

From walking the gymnast can progress into small running steps. This should be done with the weight on the balls of the feet and the legs straight much of the time. The running must be continued until there is no loss of balance and the gymnast feels quite confident. Following this the gymnast should practise leaps along the beam. Two leaps should be performed from one end of the beam to the other, with one step in between. These must be practised many times so that the courage and confidence of the gymnast increases. The leaps must become longer and higher and show a greater mastery of technique: the legs well split, the head held high, and lightness and control on landing.

When these leaps have been practised sufficiently time can be spent on agilities. These will vary according to the gymnast's ability. In the very early stages she will finish her warm-up by performing leaps. As she goes on to perform a voluntary exercise, however, she will spend time in practising the individual components, such as rolls, handstands and cartwheels. As in the case of leaps, the first cartwheel practised in a training session may be poor. Repetitions of this movement should bring an increase in confidence and, it is to be hoped, an improved performance. If all basic floorwork has been correctly mastered, the perfected skill has only to be transferred to the beam, following the usual progression. If the movement is not familiar then the best way to learn it is to get off the beam and try it on the floor, then the bench, then the floor beam.

Working several gymnasts on the beam

It is vital that the gymnast spends as much time on the beam as possible. In thirty minutes six gymnasts are only going to get five minutes each on the beam. Obviously it is much better if you can have two or more beams. However, the gymnasts can rotate round the other apparatus (bench and floor beam) so that all can be working throughout the thirty minutes. Gymnasts must get used to working beam by themselves with the coach just commenting from the side. The gymnast should very rarely need a stand-in. When transferring a difficult skill from the floor beam to the high beam it is better that the gymnast utilizes crash mats and places them under the beam rather than have the coach stand in. The mats can then be taken away one at a time. With a limited number of crash mats in the gym other apparatus can be placed under the crash mat to raise it; sometimes trestle tables are available or benches placed side by side.

With basic skills six gymnasts can work on one beam together (fig. 135). This is assuming that they have had a good grounding in floor skills and that the movements set out below have previously been learnt on the floor.

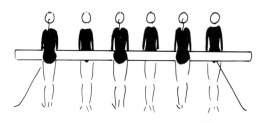

135

Mounting the beam

1 They can all jump to front support (fig. 143).

2 They can squat on. This can be done by jumping and lifting the seat as shown in fig. 144. The arms must be kept straight and the gymnast must jump off two feet as with the front support. Then get the gymnasts to squat on (fig. 145). Notice that the shoulders need to go forwards when squatting on the beam.

3 Taking off from two feet the gymnasts can squat through to back support. The body should be straight as shown in fig. 146, with the head up and the shoulders down. The feet should not touch the beam on the squat through.

4 Squat one leg through. This is done with a two-footed take-off. The legs must be well split and straight as shown in fig. 147.

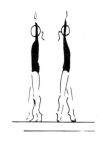

136

Activities on the beam

1 All six gymnasts can half turn. The feet should be placed one in front of the other. With the arms in ring position above the head the gymnasts rise right up on the balls of the feet and half turn (fig. 136). This can be repeated several times.

2 Jumps can be done from the same starting position as above. The feet must be turned outwards with the balls of the feet on the beam and the heels slightly over the side of the beam. Simple jumps can be done as shown or the feet can be changed in the air (fig. 137).

3 The arabesque can be practised. The gymnasts will need to balance on the same leg and turn at a slight angle across the beam, to the right if balancing on the right foot. In fig. 138 the gymnast lifts the free leg to as near the horizontal as she can manage. The back should be kept upright (fig. 138b). She should feel a pinch in the middle of the back. Still lifting the leg she can then lower the body slightly in order for the leg to go higher (fig. 138c). The arms in this instance are held out to the side. This position should be held for two seconds and then the gymnast needs to return to the starting position by reversing the order of movements shown.

137

Standing up on beam

After some mounts or rolls the gymnast finds herself in front support or sitting across the beam. Obviously she needs to come up to standing without having to climb on the apparatus and to show a degree of gymnastic skill.

a   b   c   138

71

Standing from front support

This is the simplest way of coming up to standing. The gymnast lifts one leg over the beam, taking the weight on her hands, and quarter turns to come to astride sitting. From this position she lifts both her legs, keeping them straight, into a V sit (fig. 139a). After showing this position for half a second she then bends one leg and places the foot on the beam. Reaching forwards with the arms and free leg she can then stand up. Notice that when the gymnast is in the V sit position the hands are behind the hips holding on to the beam. The pike of the V must be close (fig. 139b).

Standing from a forward roll

The exit from a roll is very similar to the previous movement. As the gymnast comes to sitting she must bend one leg, placing the foot on the beam, and reach forwards with the free leg and arms (see fig. 150).

Standing from astride sitting

A gymnast often arrives in astride sitting as she did from front support in fig. 140a. One of the requirements for competitive gymnastics is that movements are not repeated in another part of the exercise. Having done a V sit to stand up the gymnast needs some alternatives for variation. The following method is slightly harder.

The gymnast lifts her legs to a V sit position but keeps them apart, her arms forwards and between the legs. She pauses here for a moment and then places her hands side by side on the beam as she swings the legs downwards, backwards and upwards. She must aim to get the legs together and above the horizontal on the backswing (fig. 140b). From here she should bend one leg to place one foot on the beam with the free leg outstretched behind.

Another version of this is for the gymnast to swing the legs behind her and squat both feet on to the beam, one slightly behind the other. The gymnast needs good co-ordination and strength to succeed in this movement. At a later stage the gymnast can swing to handstand (fig. 141) or swing straight into a forward roll.

There are other methods of standing up on the beam so if you discover a method which looks skilful and not too elaborate then it will be quite acceptable.

Mounts

For the start of a beam exercise a reuther board can be used as a take-off platform. This also applies to the bars.

Many mounts for the beam are taken off two feet, as with vaulting, and can show a certain amount of flight.

The jump to front support

For any mount where the gymnast has to grasp the beam she can do so in two different ways; she can keep the thumbs by the fingers as shown in fig. 142, or put the thumbs around the beam. Obviously to do the latter

139

140

141

142

she needs fairly big hands. The hands should be shoulder width apart.

Taking off from two feet she should jump to the position shown in fig. 143. This should be done from a static position; a run into a jump should not be needed for such a simple mount. The gymnast must achieve the position as shown straight away, keeping the head up, shoulders pressed down and a slight hollow or extension in the body. The legs must be together with the knees and ankles stretched.

From this position the gymnast can then lift one leg over the beam to come to astride sitting, keeping the weight on the hands and not allowing the body to sag on to the beam.

143

The squat on

A short run may be used for this mount but, as indicated on page 71, it is possible without a run.

The hands should be placed on the beam as before. With a push from the reuther board or the floor the gymnast lifts the hips keeping the legs straight and together. As she does so she must allow the shoulders to go forward beyond the beam keeping the arms straight. The legs are then bent up, placing the balls of the feet on the beam. The gymnast should then adjust her position by bringing the shoulders slightly back and either lifting her heels to take the weight forwards or dropping them to take the weight backwards. The head should be up with the shoulders sloping down. Feet and knees must be together (figs 144 and 145).

144

The squat through

This is a development of the squat on. As the gymnast bends her knees she must lift them clear of the beam to pass them over the beam so that they can straighten. The shoulders are well forwards as she makes the squat action. As the feet come over the beam and extend downwards the shoulders must move backwards. The degree of shoulder movement will be perfected by the gymnast after several attempts at this movement. Notice that when in back support (fig. 146) the shoulders are behind the beam. As with front support the head must be up, shoulders down, body slightly extended and arms, legs and ankles stretched.

145

The squat one leg through

The take-off is off two feet as previously. When the feet have left the ground then they split, one taken between the hands. This leg must then straighten to come to a forward astride sitting (fig. 147). The split of the legs must be even either side of the beam. As before, the legs must be held straight, the head held up and shoulders down.

146

The straddle on or over

The take-off is from two feet. It may be necessary to take a short run for this mount using the reuther board as a take-off platform.

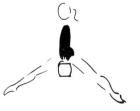

147

The legs are straddled after they leave the floor. In order to gain continuity in a beam exercise it is best that the straddle is wide so that the gymnast can go down immediately to side splits. Once side splits are achieved the hands should come off the beam and can then be held as shown in fig. 148.

148

In the straddle over (fig. 149) the gymnast must have good control. To have the thumbs around the beam will help to make this mount successful. As the legs come over the beam straddled they should be straight. Once in a position of balance the gymnast should aim to lift the feet so that they are slightly higher than the hips, keeping the legs straight. The gymnast may have to place her hands closer together than normal, particularly if she is going to turn to face down the beam. This type of turn can be developed into a three-quarter turn instead of a quarter turn, in which case the gymnast will have to cross her arms as she turns.

149

The forward roll on

This mount (fig. 150) is most easily done at the end of the beam. A reuther board is advisable as the gymnast needs to show flight before coming on to the beam. From a two-footed take-off the gymnast swings her arms forwards grasping the end of the beam as for a handstand along the beam (see fig. 151). As her hands meet the beam her shoulders should be behind the beam with the arms straight. As momentum takes her forwards she must bend her arms and tuck the head under. At this stage the legs should still be stretched horizontal. The roll must be as continuous as it would be on the floor. The hands should stay on top of the beam. As the hips come to the beam the shoulders and back should come up so that the gymnast is ready to stand by bending one leg and stretching the other. She could also come up to stand by squatting the feet on (see page 73).

150

Practise this mount first on the end of a box. If the coach needs to stand in on the first attempts she should stand in as for a forward roll along the beam.

151

The shoulder stand

This mount (fig. 152) is quite easily learnt providing the gymnast has good body tension. It is taken from two feet, using a reuther board if necessary. The hands are placed on the beam as for a handstand across the beam. The gymnast jumps lifting the seat so that she passes through a pike position. It is also possible to do this lift through a straddle position. The weight is taken on the hands only; the shoulders should not rest on the beam. The gymnast must start with the arms bent and must lift the hips immediately.

To come out of this movement the gymnast can either split the legs and come down to one side coming on to one knee or she can hollow the body slightly and by lifting the shoulders forwards and upwards can come to front support with the arms straight.

152

Handstand mounts

The handstand on the end of the beam can be practised first on the box. As with the shoulder stand, the gymnast can either straddle or pike up to the handstand.

The coach can stand in for the first attempts, placing the near hand under the gymnast's stomach and the far hand on the gymnast's back. The gymnast can either go into a forward roll, a forward walk-over or a turn on the hands to cartwheel walk-out. It may be necessary to put two boxes together to get the full sequence of movements.

Having practised the movement by herself the gymnast can then try it on the beam. The coach should limit the amount of standing in that she does. The gymnast should now be completely familiar with the movement and should have enough control to carry it out unaided.

The distance of the reuther board away from the beam will vary. For the pike up the board may be in fairly close but for the straddle the board needs to be a little closer.

The handstand can also be done across the beam. This can be practised straight away on the beam. Three gymnasts could practise this at once if they are arranged on alternate sides and there are sufficient mats and three reuther boards. If the gymnast overbalances then she should turn out of the handstand to land on the other side of the beam.

She can come out of the handstand in several ways (see page 78).

Mounts from one foot

These mounts are usually done from the side of the beam with a diagonal approach. The simplest of these is shown in fig. 153. As the gymnast approaches the beam the near hand is placed on the beam and the near foot is swung forwards and upwards over the beam to the riding seat position as shown. The second leg pushes from the floor and is then swung over the beam.

153

For this and other one-footed mounts the coach can give support by grasping the gymnast's free hand and the armpit.

From the side the gymnast can mount on to one foot using one hand as a support on the beam or she can mount just using the foot so that she comes immediately to standing.

A free mount on to one foot can also be done on to the end of the beam or across the beam from the side.

Beam skills

Most of these skills are performed exactly as described in Chapter 2. However, it is worth repeating the following: skills should not be taught on the beam; they must progress to it by the easy stages listed on page 69. Standing in should be kept to a minimum.

The forward roll

The forward roll on the beam should be as near as possible to what it would be on the floor. The gymnast usually starts with the feet together and then reaches well forward and continues through the roll without stopping. The legs must be straight as they leave the beam. The hands will go side by side on the beam (see fig. 151) as for handstands along the beam. The usual way for the gymnast to stand up out of the roll is by stepping out as shown in fig. 150.

If the gymnast needs a stand-in for the first attempt on the high beam it can be done in the following manner.

The coach stands at the side of the beam and in front of the gymnast in squat position. The coach should then reach out with her near hand and hold the gymnast at the top of the arm by turning the palm upwards and holding the arm between the Y-shape of the thumb and the fingers. As the gymnast rolls the shoulder will drop into the coach's palm. As she begins the roll the coach should hold on to the gymnast's hips or waist at the side only with the far hand. It does help considerably if the gymnast has track trousers on so that the coach has something to hold. The coach must then be ready to move along the beam with the gymnast and not give support unless it is necessary.

It is not advisable for the gymnast to practise a forward roll on the floor beam or a low beam. If she falls off this apparatus whilst rolling forwards she invariably finishes up lying across the edge of the beam with the sharp edge of the beam sticking into her back. It is much more comfortable to fall from a high beam in the roll.

The backward roll

This is done exactly the same as on the floor. The gymnast should aim to lift the hips as she does on the floor.

If the coach needs to stand in she should stand to the side and in front of the gymnast. As the gymnast rolls backwards the coach should move closer in and grasp the hips as they leave the beam, one hand either side using the grip between the thumb and the fingers. The coach is then in an ideal position to help the gymnast by lifting the hips and guiding her feet on to the beam if necessary. With this method the gymnast does need to have the confidence to do the first part of the roll by herself. It does help, however, if she can see the coach moving in as she rolls backwards.

The handstand

The handstand can be done along the beam or across the beam. In the former the gymnast steps in to the handstand as she would on the floor. The hands are placed side by side as shown in fig. 151, with the fingers reaching down the side of the beam. A great deal of practice is needed by the gymnast to perfect this balance on such a narrow base. Work on the floor beam is very valuable here. There is a slight tendency for the head to

Above A dive cartwheel on the beam (Tourischeva, USSR).

Left A straddle to handstand which can be used in mounting the beam (Tourischeva, USSR).

be lifted higher than in a handstand on the floor. This is due to the arms being so close that space is restricted. It may help the gymnast to look along the beam rather than downwards. The gymnast comes down from the handstand as she would on the floor although looking down more to spot the beam as the first foot comes in close to the hands (see fig. 154).

154

The handstand can also be done across the beam. It is more difficult for the gymnast to get to the handstand, but once there it is easier for her to balance. This can be practised first of all on the floor. The gymnast should face front and step forward as if going into a handstand. As she reaches down to the ground she should turn the hands and the body to the side. The hands should reach the floor one slightly after the other. As the second hand touches the gymnast should push away from this to help to stop rotation and ensure that she arrives in the handstand (fig. 155) and does not continue out as for a cartwheel. She must also make sure that she does not swing the first leg too hard. The hands must be shoulder width apart and pointing forwards as they would be in a handstand approached from the straight position.

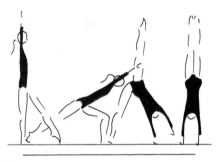

155

Having done this several times with success on a line the gymnast should try using the bench and then the floor beam. On both these pieces the gymnast must allow the fingers to go down the side of the apparatus so that she is gripping the beam or bench.

Before attempting this skill on the high beam the gymnast needs to know how to come out of the handstand if she overbalances. It is fairly straightforward to come out of the handstand by piking and returning to the ground but if she overbalances the other way it presents more problems. With the gymnast on the bench or box top the coach should stand in so that she supports the hips from the back of the gymnast. In the case of the gymnast in fig. 156 the last hand to go down on to the bench was the right. The coach should then grasp hold of the gymnast's right wrist with her left hand, the right still being on the gymnast's hip. The coach then lifts the gymnast's hand up off the bench and turns her to the left, allowing the hips to turn and the legs to pike down to the floor. The coach lifts the hand up thus helping to bring the gymnast to a standing position.

The gymnast needs to feel slightly overbalanced as she goes into this turn. When doing this on the high beam the gymnast should not pike but try and keep the body straight, as in fig. 156. Although this has been introduced as a safety movement this can also be a dismount.

As with all handstands on the beam it is very important that the gymnast has a proper understanding of the handstand and good body tension. If the gymnast cannot hold the handstand for a second on the beam without collapsing then she should not be doing it and the coach should not be 'manhandling' her through the move.

Once the gymnast has mastered the balance on the beam she can try different ways of coming down from the handstand. The handstand across the beam offers more variety.

156

Above The hands are about to take the gymnast's weight on the beam in a back flip from backward walk-over (Ungureanu, Romania).

Left above Beginning the push from the front for a backward walk-over . . . and (*below*) maintaining the tension in this flowing movement (Filatova, USSR).

Fig. 157 shows the gymnast coming down from the handstand in a straddle. The gymnast needs to be supple and have good control. The wider the gymnast can straddle the legs the less strength needed. Notice in fig. 157c how the hips have moved over the shoulders so that there is a slight hollow in the back. As the gymnast brings her legs round to the straddle support in fig. 157d the gymnast must move the shoulders back from the forward position as seen in b and c. This should be practised on the floor first.

From a split position in the handstand across the beam the gymnast can turn the body and come down as shown in fig. 158. Here the gymnast has her left leg forwards in the split and the right backwards. She then turns the forward leg towards the right thus turning all the body. Notice how

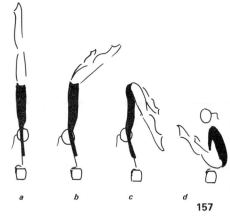

a   b   c   d

157

158

the left leg turns across the body. The hands remain still on the beam so that the arms cross as the turn is made. The coming down is therefore similar to the end of the cartwheel except that the opposite leg is used. It is possible at a more advanced stage to walk around on the hands with the legs in splits before coming up. Grozdova from the USSR was perfection at this. Her complete beam exercise was out of this world.

The handstand roll
A fairly obvious way of coming out of a handstand along the beam is for the gymnast to roll. This is done exactly as it is on the floor. It is best to use the bent arm roll on the beam. It is important that the gymnast does not stop in this movement and try and grab the beam; she must roll continuously as she would on the floor. As with forward rolls it is not advisable to practise this on the floor beam. The gymnast comes up as she would from a roll (fig. 159).

159

The cartwheel
There is a lot of discussion about the cartwheel on the beam. Many people say that it should be done completely sideways as it is first taught on the floor. The sideways cartwheel is very static on the beam and is very difficult. I feel that the cartwheel on the beam should be treated as a linking movement. I recommend that the cartwheel is taught from the

160

forward position, turning in to finish (fig. 160). The gymnast should still keep the same qualities that are demanded in a cartwheel, that is, continuity and extension. The hands should still go down one slightly after the other. By turning the cartwheel in at the end it becomes an ideal movement to lead into the backward walk-over or to change direction. It should not be treated as a difficult move and it should never be supported. If the gymnast cannot do a good cartwheel on the floor beam there is no way that she will do it on the high beam.

The backward walk-over
This is the same as for the floor, the only difference being that the gymnast has to place her hands side by side as she would in a handstand along the beam. The gymnast must make sure that her technique is correct; her back should be straight as soon as she gets into the handstand and her legs well split (fig. 161). It may be necessary for the coach to stand in for one or two attempts. The coach stands behind the gymnast facing her and places her hands round the waist using the fingers and thumb to grip. When standing on the left side of the gymnast she should put the left hand on the far side of the gymnast and the right hand on the near side. Obviously the gymnast needs lots of practice, particularly on the low apparatus. When going into the backward walk-over the gymnast must not hesitate but must aim for continuity out of her previous movement.

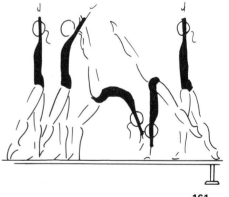

161

One way of practising the backward walk-over very early on is for the gymnast to use a bench as shown in fig. 162. The gymnast should push up to bridge with her hands at the end of the bench. From here she can then kick over to the floor and there is no fear of her hitting the apparatus. Both ends of the bench can be utilized in this way at the same time.

As soon as the backward walk-over is mastered the gymnast needs to practise joining two together or linking a cartwheel to a backward walk-over. These movements must be practised so that there is no pause between one and the other. This calls for complete stretch and body tension.

162

The forward walk-over

This movement is done exactly the same as it is on the floor. As with all walk-overs on the beam the gymnast does need to be more supple in the shoulders than she would for success on the floor. With the hands close together on the beam the range of movement in the shoulder joint is limited. There is a tendency to hollow the back too much in order to keep the eyes on the beam for as long as possible. This is not the ideal movement. The gymnast must practise many times so that she will be confident and maintain tension and stretch within the body. As with the backward walk-over the forward one should be done linking it with another or any other agility on the beam.

The back flip

The back flip on the beam can be done in two slightly different ways, as a move by itself or as a movement following the backward walk-over or cartwheel. The back flip that I have described on the floor (see page 40) does not have a preliminary arm swing. When performing a back flip by itself this is needed. Some coaches decide not to bother about the single back flip as it is not such a good beam element as the flip from a backward walk-over. However, you cannot always train to such high standards unless you are presented with ideal type gymnasts.

Now that the gymnast has mastered the flip on the floor from the round-off she will very easily learn the preceding arm swing. Obviously, first attempts are done on the floor. From standing with the feet together the gymnast bends the knees as if sitting in a chair and swings the arms backwards just behind the hips. In this off balance state she then swings the arms forwards and backwards whilst straightening the legs to jump backward into the flip. Because of the nature of the beam and the need to flow from one movement to the other the legs should split as they leave the floor. It is important that the back leg trails slightly to slow down the flip and the return to the beam. The donkey action typical of the flip on the floor is not present. The last phase of the back flip on the beam is more typical of the exit from a backward walk-over, one leg coming down after the other as in fig. 163.

163

Having practised this on the floor the gymnast can then progress to a line, then the bench and floor beam. It is useful at the floor beam stage to build the floor up to the level of the beam (fig. 164). It is also advisable to have some sort of covering over the wooden beam. A length of carpet can be wrapped round the beam and tacked on underneath.

164

Some advice may need to be given to the gymnast as to how she places her hands on the beam. To place them side by side as in a backward walk-over is not advisable. They can be placed in several ways, one in front of the other or with the hands turned in as shown in fig. 165. Some gymnasts even place one hand on top of the other. None of these are incorrect and the gymnast can use the one she likes best.

165

At any of these stages the gymnast may need support, but it is not good to stand in too much. The gymnast must conquer her fear and progress slowly using as many stages as possible. Even on the high beam attempts should be done alone; crash mats can be put under the beam or a platform built up with boxes or tables or benches. The support, when needed, is very simple. The coach stands at the side and towards the back of the gymnast shown in fig. 166, and places her near hand on the gymnast's waist at the back, with the back of the hand against the body. As the gymnast swings the arms and extends the body the coach can turn the hand slightly so that she is now supporting under the waist with the palm of the hand. The second hand then comes on to the gymnast's stomach as soon as the arms have swung backwards. The coach should maintain the hold until the gymnast has come to her feet and brought the arms above the head. This support can be used even if the coach is low down and the gymnast is up on the beam.

166

The back flip from backward walk-over

This back flip, often referred to as a back handspring or fly flip, is higher than the previous flip. From the backward walk-over the feet come down one at a time on to the balls of the feet. The arms are then lifted up quickly with the body to jump upwards and backwards into the flip. You should be able to see from fig. 167 the difference in take-off from the orthodox flip. Here the gymnast is more on balance at point of take-off, whereas with the normal flip the gymnast must be off balance. The gymnast comes down on to the feet one at a time as in the standing back flip. The movement is more spectacular than the standing flip as the gymnast moves straight into it without a pause, one foot slightly behind the other from the backward walk-over. The added height makes the movement more elegant.

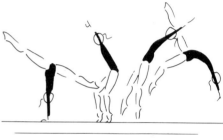

167

The gymnast should practise first on the floor and then progress to the bench and floor beam, etc.

For supporting the coach will stand in as before but she must follow the walk-over through using just the near hand on the gymnast's back. This can be kept there all the time from walk-over through to flip. The second hand supports only in the flip. As with all movements on the beam the support should be as light as possible and in no way must the coach impede the movement.

Dismounts

The simplest form of dismount from the beam is a vertical jump. There are several rules that need to be observed.
1 The gymnast must get height from the beam and not just drop off.
2 She must show extension before she makes any change in body shape.

3 She must maintain good body tension and obviously show good style in the shape being performed.

4 She must show good extension before landing, reaching slightly forwards with the feet to compensate for the forward momentum.

5 Landing must be under control, with quick recovery. Some of the jumps that can be used are as follows: straight (fig. 168), star (fig. 169), straddle (fig. 170) and tuck (fig. 171).

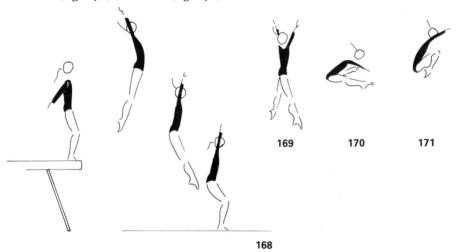

169   170   171

168

The cartwheel dismount

The cartwheel from the end of the beam is an ideal first inverted dismount (fig. 172). The gymnast stands facing the end of the beam. She steps forwards and turns her hands as for a cartwheel so that the fingers are down the side of the beam. The second hand should be at the end of the beam. As the gymnast passes through the vertical the second leg must join the first. The gymnast then continues to wheel out and land sideways to the beam. This is the only movement where I would advise the gymnast to land sideways from a height and stand still. (Cartwheel vaults can cause a lot of knee problems.) The tendency is for the gymnast to want to turn inwards as she lands. She must keep her last arm firmly out to the side pressing away from the beam.

   The coach may need to stand in for first attempts. She should stand on the back side of the gymnast; if the gymnast cartwheels with the left hand leading then the coach stands on the left side of the gymnast. With the nearest hand the coach should hold the gymnast on the left side of the hip. As the gymnast begins to invert the left hand should go to the right side of the hip. If the beam is very high and the coach short, it may be difficult to use this hold. I would then advise the beam to be lowered, as it is important to get the first hand on to the gymnast's hips early. When the gymnast lands the coach should still be supporting the gymnast with her arms now crossed.

172

84

The half cartwheel to handstand quarter turn out
This is another description of the movement shown in fig. 156.

The round-off
This dismount is almost the same as the cartwheel. As the gymnast comes to the vertical she makes a quarter turn inwards to face the beam. The hands will leave the beam together (fig. 173). The coach stands in as for the cartwheel. With the first attempt the gymnast may just drop off but as she becomes more confident she should aim to get flight off the hands so that the body is nearly straight in flight.

173

The free cartwheel or Barani dismount
The first requirement for the gymnast who wishes to do this dismount is to be able to do the free cartwheel on the floor.

Now she has to learn a slightly different shape for the free cartwheel off the beam. Her first step is to do the round-off. With the round-off she will end facing the beam. Having established this the coach should then take her for a free cartwheel on the floor so that the legs join at the vertical and the gymnast lands turned inwards. The coach has to be prepared to support quite well particularly for the last phase. If she thinks that she cannot cope with this then it would be better if the gymnast worked from the end of the bench or a reuther board.

After several repetitions the gymnast should then progress to the beam. The coach should stand in as she did for the free cartwheel for the floor, see page 39. It is important to get the near hand on to the gymnast's hip before she leaves the beam to give her confidence (fig. 174).

As with the free cartwheel on the floor the gymnast must take a long step with the foot stepping to the end of the beam. The gymnast must drive hard off the last leg, swinging (in the case of the gymnast in fig. 174) her left arm downwards, backwards and upwards. The gymnast should try and achieve a straight position when in flight. Notice how the arms are to the sides and not hanging down below the head when the gymnast is inverted.

174

A common fault with this dismount is that the gymnast drops off the beam and pikes in to land. Not only will this technique lose a lot of marks but it indicates that the gymnast is not ready for this movement.

The cartwheel back somersault dismount
The gymnast needs to be able to perform a good back somersault on the floor before performing this dismount. So often gymnasts and coaches think that it is easy to do somersault dismounts from the beam even though the gymnast cannot do them on the floor. It is not enough to fall from the beam and turn over in the air. The gymnast must show height from the beam with a back somersault and, as for the floor, show extension, tuck and extension before landing.

First the gymnast must practise the cartwheel. This can be done on the bench or floor. From facing front the gymnast steps into the cartwheel, turning in to finish and landing one foot behind the other, but still bringing the feet down one, two, as for a cartwheel. She must finish on the balls of the feet with the knees slightly bent. From here she can jump backwards on to a crash mat (fig. 175). The arms must stay by the ears all the time so that there is no intermediate swing. It is important that the leading foot comes in close to the hands making it easy for the gymnast to stand up quickly. She does not use a push off the hands as in the round-off; the first foot touches the ground whilst the hands are still on the floor.

175　　　　　　　　　　　　　　　　　　　　　　　**176**

The next stage is for the gymnast to do a back somersault off the bench starting with one foot in front of the other. The coach should stand in for this.

Then the gymnast can join both movements together. The arms must lift from the cartwheel straight upwards and backwards into the stretch prior to the tuck position in the somersault. The more the gymnast stretches as she leaves the bench the higher the somersault will go.

When she has achieved success after several repetitions from the bench she can go to the beam. She may have to break the movement down again, that is, a cartwheel and a jump and then the back somersault, etc. When her confidence has increased with the whole sequence she must then begin to attack the cartwheel with a bit more speed. This should give more height to the somersault and therefore more time to open up before the landing (fig. 176). One problem that may arise when the gymnast performs this off the beam is that she could be too close to the beam as she dismounts. Check that she has enough backward movement to keep her clear of the beam with her head.

The Gainer back somersault

With this somersault the gymnast moves forwards before going into the back somersault. The actual somersault is taken from a one-foot take-off.

First, as always, the gymnast must break the movement down. Use a bench and a crash mat. The coach should always test the crash mat before use, particularly in this type of dismount. If the mat is the type that will 'bottom' easily, in other words, the gymnast lands on to the floor because the mat is not thick enough, then another thin mat should be placed on top of the crash mat. This will spread the load. Or, two crash mats should be used, one on top of the other.

The gymnast must establish which foot she would like to somersault from. If she has decided on the left then she should stand on the bench and swing the right leg forwards and upwards so that she lifts off the bench and lands on her back on the crash mat, which should be on the right side of the bench. As she steps in she should swing her arms forwards and upwards. The coach must then make sure that she uses the left foot and does jump off it (fig. 177).

177

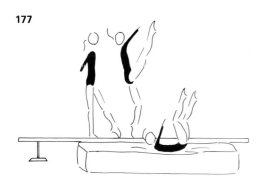

178

After several practices jumping from one foot the gymnast can then try the back somersault. This can either be done on the floor or from the bench. The coach will need to stand in supporting under the back and lifting the hips with the other hand. When this is good and the gymnast is confident she can then try from the beam (fig. 178). On first attempt it is best if two or three mats are placed one on top of the other so that the gymnast is landing on a high platform. The coach should stand at the side of the crash mats to stop the gymnast falling off the mats on landing or to give some support if necessary; this is quite difficult as the coach will have to stand on the mats which are very unstable. If too much support is needed the gymnast should take the somersault back to the bench.

In the somersault the gymnast must tuck from the stretched jump and aim to open up before landing as she would in a back somersault on the floor. If the gymnast only drops off the beam then more work must be done with the step, swinging the free leg and landing on the back.

The front somersault dismount
Once again this dismount can be practised first of all on low apparatus. A reuther board or bench can be used as a take-off platform. The arm swing can be practised in a static situation. The gymnast should stand with one foot in front of the other with the arms downwards and backwards behind

the body. As the gymnast swings the arms forwards and upwards (the same action as used in the vault) she should swing the back leg backwards and rise off the front foot, straightening the knee without bringing the front foot off the ground (fig. 179).

179

When this pattern is established the gymnast can try the front somersault. The coach needs to stand just in front of the apparatus, ready to support. As the gymnast lifts the arms the coach must place her near hand or arm across the gymnast's stomach and the far hand on the gymnast's back to help lift and turn her over. The coach must make sure that she does not come in too soon with the first hand so that the arm swing is stopped. The gymnast must swing the back leg hard and drive off the front leg. As the gymnast extends out of the jump the arms will have reached upwards and forwards but they must be pulled downwards and backwards quickly to assist rotation as the gymnast tucks. She must anticipate landing and open out early to stop over-rotation. She must land with both feet together so the legs need to join in the somersault (fig. 180).

180

One of the common faults is that the gymnast swings the arms forwards only and not upwards, and this determines the height of the somersault. Another fault is that the gymnast forgets to bring the arms back having swung them forwards.

Before attempting this dismount off the beam the gymnast must try it on her own off the board or bench using a few steps into the somersault. If this is successful it can then be done off the beam with the coach standing by to stop the gymnast over-rotating, which she is quite likely to do on her first attempt from a height.

Links for floor and beam

As stated earlier on in this chapter, floor and beam require similar skills. This is the same for the links although some of the links may be possible only on the floor.

For a complete exercise on either piece of apparatus the gymnast is required to show movements on low, medium and high levels. Various types of rolls come in to the first category.

Rolls

As well as rolling forwards and backwards it is possible to roll sideways and to incorporate various types of roll to make a short sequence (beware of a tendency to go mad on the rolling theme and too much time being spent on the floor).

1 The gymnast should be stretched out on her back and then roll over on to her front and continue on to her back. The degree of roll can vary, anything from 180 to 540 degrees. To get out of this movement the gymnast could roll back or forwards to stand or sit.

181

2 This roll (fig. 181) from the knees over the shoulders and back to the knees can be considered similar to a cartwheel.

3 This very simple roll over one shoulder (fig. 182) could be performed after a half roll forwards to sit and then back over the shoulder to kneeling before standing up.

182

183

Balances

Positions of balance are usually held slightly longer on the beam than on the floor, when the gymnast usually only passes through the movement.

On one leg

1 The most obvious movement here is the arabesque, which can be held at various levels. Fig. 183 shows the leg horizontal. The body must be nearly vertical, so not only must the gymnast be very supple but also very strong in the back and seat muscles (gluteals). The arms can be held in various ways but they must in some way form a line with the rest of the gymnast. Fig. 184 shows an arabesque with a bent leg support.

184

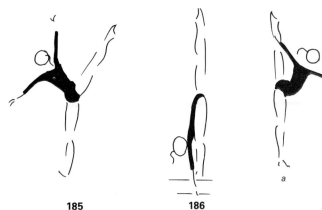

188

185   **186**   **187**

189

190

2 The side balance (fig. 185) was made famous by the Russian gymnast, Grozdova.

3 The needle stand (fig. 186).

4 The leg can also be held up with one or both hands at the front and the back (fig. 187).

On the hands

1 The handstand can be held in various ways: stag (fig. 188), split (fig. 189) and oblique split (fig. 190), again made famous by Grozdova.

2 The piked or Russian lever (fig. 191).

3 The straddle lever shown in the handstand on the beam (see fig. 157).

Splits

The technique for the splits has been covered in Chapter 1 (see page 14, hip joint exercise no. 12).

On the floor exercise it is more usual for the gymnast to move through splits than stay there. Often a gymnast will move into a roll or turn forwards on to her front as shown in fig. 192.

Whether on beam or floor there is nothing worse than a slow slide into splits. The movement must show ease and artistry. Various walk-overs and cartwheels can be taken into splits. In the cartwheel to splits the gymnast has to keep the hips high as the first leg is brought across in front of the body and arms to come to splits. Notice in fig. 193 how one hand is brought off the floor whilst the other remains there.

191

192

193

194

Leaps

Leaps are springs from the feet taking off one foot after the other. The most common leap is a grand jeté in which the gymnast leaves the floor stretching one leg forwards and one backwards (fig. 194). The landing is on the front leg (one foot only). It is important that the arms are held well, the opposite arm to the front leg forwards and the other held out to the side. The head must be held up and the shoulders kept down. Notice that on landing the back leg is still held up and the arms and back are up.

Split leap

This leap is often used on the beam. It does allow the gymnast to use up only a short distance and also get the legs into splits. The front leg is bent before it is lifted forwards and the back leg takes off from the ground almost as soon as the front leg. With this leap it is all right for the arms to be held out to the side.

Leap with back leg bent

Again the gymnast takes off one foot behind the other. Obviously to make the most of this sort of leap (fig. 195) the gymnast must be supple in the back leg and the back. The arms can be held above the head or opposite arm forwards and the other arm above the head. The leap can also be done as a jump, that is off two feet and landing on two feet.

195

196

a   b   c   d   e   f

Turning leap

The gymnast starts as she would for a straight leap. Having swung the first leg forward the gymnast then makes a half turn, to the right if she is swinging the left (fig. 196). As she makes the turn she must scissor kick the legs so that the left leg is now forwards and the right leg back. She then lands on the left leg. Unfortunately this leap is usually performed with a very small split of the legs as shown in fig. 196f. A judge would deduct marks for lack of amplitude if she did the movement as shown.

Jumps and hops

A jump usually refers to a spring off two feet together and landing on two feet.

As with the dismounts from the beam a jump can be stretch, tuck, star or straddle. The legs can also be in a stag position (fig. 197c). Another variation of a jump is for the back leg to be bent with the foot up behind the body and the other leg pointing straight down to the ground (fig. 197e). There are other jumps where the legs can be taken to the side and these can be varied by the bending of one or both legs. Obviously different types of jumps will suit different people; only the more supple gymnast will be able to do the jump in fig. 197e. A stiff gymnast will have to try and make as much impact by jumping higher but taking the legs to the side or forwards in a straddle where back mobility is not needed.

Fig. 198 shows a hop. The gymnast lifts one leg forwards and upwards as she jumps from the other foot. Notice that in this hop the opposite arm to the front leg is taken forwards with the other arm to the back. The gymnast lands on the straight leg. As with all other springs the variety of shapes that can be shown is numerous, one leg to the back, to the side, with both legs straight or introducing a turn.

It is essential to look for variety in every single exercise and gymnast; each has different qualities. Insist on good technique, height in jumps, good recovery before landing and then good progression into the next movement. It is often harder to learn this aspect of gymnastics than the exciting and difficult skills.

197

198

Above A variation on an arabesque in a sequence along the beam (Koval, USSR).

Above left A confident split leap (Hellmann, DDR).

Left In a stag handstand the thighs should be horizontal, as shown. Note the use of the fingers down the side of the beam (Korbut, USSR).

93

Spins

The gymnast can spin on various parts of the body, the most usual being one foot. When spinning on one foot balance and body tension are very important.

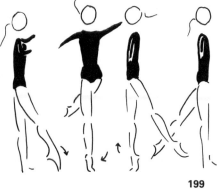

The most simple spin is one where the supporting leg is straight and the gymnast turns away from the free leg (fig. 199). All spins must be initiated somehow. In this case the gymnast pushes from the left leg as she steps on to the right and swings the right arm from the left across the body to the right. The arms are held out to the sides. The spin should be done on the ball of the foot; to stop the spin the gymnast places her heel on the floor.

199

Using this basic spin changes can be made by bending the supporting leg or back leg slightly. The arms could be held above the head. It is also possible to swing towards the back leg in which case the free leg must start in front to swing backwards to initiate the spin.

200

It is much harder to spin on one leg with the supporting leg completely bent as in fig. 200. This spin is usually used on the beam. Here the free leg must be strong as it will be lifted to the horizontal. The degree of spin can vary from 180 to 720 degrees, the latter obviously being very difficult.

Simpler spins can be done on larger areas of the body: the seat, the back of the shoulders or knees.

5 The Bars

The high and low bars, or asymmetrics, are often considered the most difficult of all girls' apparatus. On the whole the exercises required have no link with the other apparatus in the way that the beam does to the floor and as running and jumping and other natural activities are transferred to the horse. For these reasons it often takes the gymnast much longer to get used to bar work and to make any progress.

A bar exercise must be composed of predominantly swinging movements: movement from one bar to the other. Movements should not travel along the bars but should be worked in the centre to obtain maximum reaction from the bars.

Another special thing about bars is that the gymnast is working predominantly with the weight on her hands or supported by her hands. This means that her arms and shoulders must be strong. For other disciplines, such as floor vault and beam, it is mainly strength in the legs that is needed. Do not expect your gymnast to be able to cope with bar work unless she is strong in the upper body as well as the legs and hip region (see strengthening section on page 22).

Setting the width between the bars

In all high and low bars the distance between the bars is adjustable. Most modern sets of bars will have numbers on the adjuster in order that the correct distance is obtained easily. The elasticity of the 'woods' is due to their laminated composition. For beginners the distance will not matter as they will be working on one bar only; when they come to put an exercise together using both bars then the width of the bars will be vital. The width is usually tested for hip beat movements. The gymnast should lie across the low bar, hands on the top bar in ordinary grasp. She must then pike her legs under the bar so that the bar comes into the groin. She needs the bars slightly wider than this so that when she hits the bar from a long swing to hip beat she pulls the bars closer to one another in order to get maximum lift out of the bars (see fig. 238). If the bars come to her groin when at rest then she will not be able to pull the bars closer and will probably find she is hitting the bar on her hip bone. It is advisable with very small gymnasts that you compose their exercise without hip beat movements. If the bars are too close then this does not allow them to swing easily and with no wrapping movements the bars can be worked wider.

If you are just starting a gym club buying a set of high and low bars may be an impossible task for you. Very basic skills may be worked on a bar that is often found in school gyms. The bar may be quite thick; the coach should check that it is all right for use. If there is no bar available you could buy a men's horizontal bar, which is metal and has a much smaller diameter. This will probably cost half that of a set of high and low bars. A wooden bar can be fixed instead of the metal bar and it can also be made to go lower. Three or four years' work can be done on a single horizontal bar. If you are buying high and low bars make sure you get the type with guy wires and floor plates, and if possible get the best; as the gymnasts progress you may find that your bars are not suitable for advanced work.

The use of the hands on the bar

If a girl works on the bars regularly she will find that the skin of her hands becomes hard and split. To help prevent this hand-straps should be worn from the beginning so that she becomes used to them and is able to use them at all times. The hand-straps must be small so that when wearing them she cannot stretch her hand out flat. If they are too large they will ruckle when the hands are round the bar. When holding the bar the hands must be strong but at the same time gripping fairly freely to allow easy rotation.

To stop the hands becoming sticky with perspiration 'chalk' (magnesium carbonate) is used by the gymnast. It is put on the hands before the start of an exercise and when needed in practice. Beginners should not need a great deal, as they are usually on the bars for short periods only.

Ordinary or over grasp

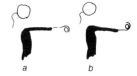

a   b   **201**

In general this grasp (fig. 201a) is used in all backward circling movements and support positions. The thumbs are usually held forward with the fingers, because of the smallness of a girl's hand and the thickness of the bar. At the beginning of a mount or for squat positions the thumbs are often held back to give greater support and balance.

Reverse or under grasp

For most forward circling movements the hands are held in reverse grasp (fig. 201b). The thumbs are held forward only momentarily at the beginning of the movement and then taken back.

Mixed grasp

This is where one hand is in over grasp and one hand in under grasp. This happens as a result of a turn.

Dislocated grasp

Here the gymnast is hanging below the bar and her hands are in a reverse grasp. Obviously the hands are wider than usual on this grasp unless the gymnast is very supple in the shoulders. This grasp is mainly used in the wrap to catch.

Shifting the grasp

In full circling and half circling movements it is necessary to move the hands round the bar. This art of shifting the grasp may determine the success or failure of a circle. I sometimes refer to the wrists being brought on top of the bar. This can apply to the reverse grasp position or to the ordinary grasp. To acquire this skill it is a great help to perform the exercise of swinging on the low bar (see below). In the early stages co-ordination between the movement of the body and that of the hands may not be very good, but this will come with practice.

Warm-up and simple activities

These simple activities or exercises should be used in the very beginning before the gymnast is able to move on to the advanced work. Several of them can also be used as a warm-up for more advanced gymnasts.

Swinging on the low bar

The main aim of this activity (fig. 202) is to teach the gymnast how to swing by using the whole body, but at the same time to relax whilst swinging. The arms must be kept straight and the shoulders relaxed so that the arms are extended to their fullest. Any swinging movement on

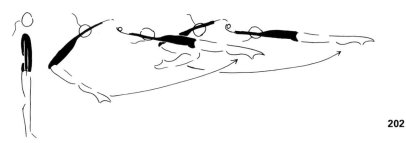

202

the bars must appear effortless. Unnecessary tension, in the shoulders for instance, will not give this impression. At the back of the swing she should try to re-grasp the bar almost like a jump-off. This ensures that the gymnast always has a good strong grip, and teaches her to shift her grasp and bring her wrists nearer to the top of the bar when necessary.

The swinging activity should be repeated as many times as possible before coming off the bar as it is also a good strengthening exercise.

Half inverted hang

Hang on the low bar and lift both legs between the hands to half inverted hand, as shown in fig. 203. Maintain this position, then come down either by continuing back or going forward again. This is a good body-awareness exercise for seat circles.

203

Undershoot from ground

The gymnast should hold on to the low bar in ordinary grasp with arms straight, shoulders down and one leg behind the other (fig. 204). A tall girl should stand further away than a short girl. Swing the back leg through

204

straight to bring the toes to the bar. The second leg pushes from the ground and then swings up to join the first at the bar. The toes then rise up beyond the bar, aiming for the top bar. The arms must be kept straight all the time. Notice how the hips are brought up to bar level before the hollow-off. The main point to remember is that the hips must be kept behind the bar as long as possible. The weight of the hips coming under the bar increases the swing and will therefore help to increase the height and length of the hollow-off. On landing the head and arms must be kept in line with the body.

Once this has been mastered from a one-footed take-off it should be executed from a spring with the feet together. The feet need to be nearer to the bar for this. Again the hips must be kept behind the bar. This activity should be practised many times as it prepares the gymnast for more advanced skills.

Front support

If the gymnasts are very small you may need to lower the bar. With the hands in ordinary grasp the gymnast should jump on to the bar as shown in fig. 205. The hands should be shoulder width apart. The shoulders must be pressed down; this may be difficult at first if the gymnast is not very strong. The bar should be resting at the top of the thigh and not in the groin. The seat muscles should be tensed so that there is a slight arch in the body with the legs straight and together. Although basic it is important that this position is perfect; you will see that many movements start from this position.

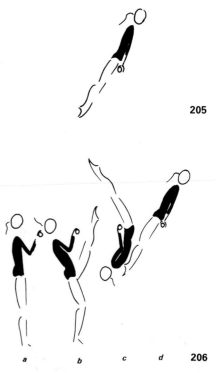

205

The upward circle

With the hands in ordinary grasp the gymnast stands with her feet just under the bar. Leaving one leg on the ground she swings the other up and over the bar, aiming to get her groin to the bar (fig. 206). The last foot then pushes off the ground and is also swung over. In the position shown in fig. 206c she must then be ready to change her grasp and bring the wrists on top of the bar to come to front support as shown in fig. 206d. She must not allow the legs to swing under the bar before arriving at this final position.

a   *b*   *c*   *d*   **206**

98

Above A straight leg squat or stoop over the bar before swinging forwards (Shaposhnikova, USSR).

Above left Piking to the bar in an upstart (Shaposhnikova, USSR).

Left The hands and toes should be placed well round the bar when circling backwards after a straddle on (Dando, GB).

Preparation lay away from front support

In order to initiate nearly every movement from the front support the gymnast has to make an action to create a reaction. This movement of action and reaction from front support must be practised as a single skill although later it is not used as such but as a vital part of many movements.

Due to the nature of the human body, the gymnast in front support rests on the bar with her thighs and not her groin. Only if she had short arms in relation to her body would the bar be at her groin. In order to swing away an action has to be made, an opposite action, so the gymnast must swing the legs under the bar to move into a pike position. If she keeps her arms straight, however, it is almost impossible to do this as the legs will not bend at the thigh. She must bend the arms in order to bring the bar to the groin (fig. 207b). The shoulders will also go forwards as shown in fig. 207b and the back will be rounded. From this position she then has to swing the legs backwards and straighten the arms as in fig. 207c and then return to the bar to come to pike again and repeat. When a gymnast first tries this practice she will probably have trouble getting her hips away from the bar. To do this she must improve her strength and body tension. She must understand that she has to open the body from the shoulder joint and not from the waist or ribs. The coach should only support this movement in the very beginning to give confidence if necessary. It is no good the coach lifting the gymnast away from the bar: it will only make the coach stronger.

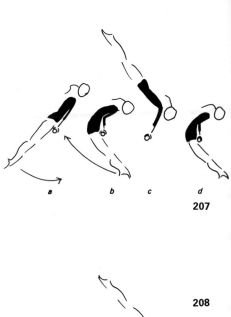

207

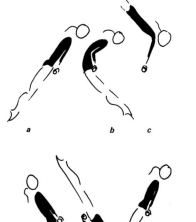

208

The backward hip circle

This movement follows on from the preparation in fig. 207. The gymnast must swing the legs under the bar as before, bending the arms sufficiently to bring the bar to the groin, and then swing away or cast. She must then return to the bar keeping the body straight and arms straight. The top of the thighs must come into the bar as the gymnast circles backwards (fig. 208d). In the beginning the coach may need to support the gymnast. She must concentrate on keeping the thighs into the bar. If the gymnast has to pike in the positions shown in figs 208e and f this means that she is not strong enough in the back and gluteals to maintain body tension. The hands must circle with the body so that the wrists come on top of the bar in the final position.

The forward hip circle

The hands are held in ordinary grasp, unlike other forward circles, where the hands are held in reverse grasp.

From the front support position there must be an extreme lift of the body from the bar, but an extended position must still be maintained. In going forward the head and chest are lifted so that the body is slightly hollow, with the bar still at the top of the thighs. When the head and shoulders have passed the horizontal and just before the inverted position there must be a sudden pike so that the body can be brought to the other side of the bar whilst the legs are still high. Maintaining this pike the gymnast circles round the bar until the position shown in fig. 209c is reached. With the shoulders forward she then swings away as shown in fig. 209d. In order to get a good hand change the gymnast should allow the wrists to go under the bar as the initial forward movement is made, since it is not until the last stage that the hand grip is really needed.

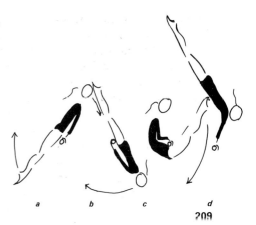

209

The undershoot from front support

This skill (fig. 210) is a preparation for the short clear circle so it is vital that the gymnast learns it correctly. It can also lead into a front somersault dismount. The gymnast from the front support lies backwards, allowing the body to circle backwards keeping the hips to the bar. There is no

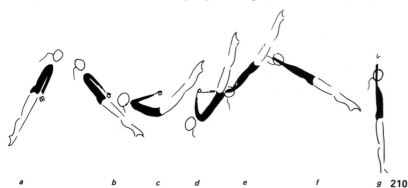

210

preparation swing as with other backward movements from front support. When she is below the bar at the horizontal she allows the hips to drop away from the bar and extend the legs upwards. This means that there must be a pike in the body with the knees coming level with the bar. As the gymnast continues to circle the top part of the body backwards she extends the feet and the hips upwards and outwards. The gymnast may need to hollow the body slightly to come to land. There is a tremendous pull through the arms forcing them away from the hips. The gymnast must be able to maintain the small angle between the arm and chest as in fig. 210c. If she opens that angle then the hips will drop too low and she will not get a high enough lift on the second side. This movement is difficult and particularly so for the girl gymnast who is not strong in the shoulder area, but it needs to be practised and learnt if she is going to progress to a good level.

Squat through to floor from front support

From a good front support position the gymnast will again need to pass her legs underneath the bar. It may be advisable for the gymnast to have her thumbs round the bar for this movement. (Many coaches say that it is wrong to work with the thumbs round the bar; I think it is up to the

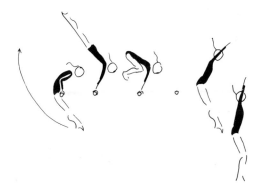

211

gymnast and the coach to work out what gives the best results.) From the swing underneath the bar (fig. 211) the gymnast swings away as before, keeping the body straight. When at the top of her swing the gymnast brings her knees forwards by bending the legs to pass them over the bar in a squat position. She must push off her hands and attempt to straighten the body before landing. The coach may need to support on first attempts. She should stand to one side of the gymnast on the landing side of the bar. She should then hold the gymnast with both hands on the near arm putting both hands above the elbow. She must then follow the gymnast through with the arms as she does the squat. Do not attempt to lift the gymnast's feet behind: if the gymnast does not get high enough for the squat then she needs to do more preparation.

The backward seat circle
Although not often used in its entirety the backward seat circle does make up parts of other movements and therefore needs to be learnt. The half inverted hang is important and needs to be well controlled. From this position the coach can come in and assist the gymnast through the last part of the circle. The gymnast's feet should go on the coach's thigh as shown in fig. 212. The gymnast then stands up, opening her body and taking care to get the wrists on top of the bar. The coach will need to walk further forwards to allow this to happen. Notice that the coach also supports with her hands on the middle of the gymnast's thighs.

212

In fig. 213a the gymnast starts with a high V position with the hips in front of the hands. This movement should be practised first on the floor. From this V hold she can then fall backwards on to the mat as she would in the first part of the circle. This can also be practised on a single floor bar. On the higher bar the gymnast can then practise the whole circle. The coach will need to stand in for the first attempts. Stand behind and to one side of the gymnast. Support her in the middle of the back and give the legs assistance if needed. Follow the gymnast round the bar with the

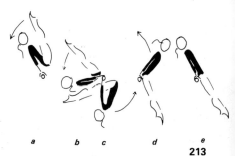

a   b   c   d   e

213

hands and on the second side either support her legs, keeping the hips to the bar, or help lift her shoulders to straighten out. This movement is so different to anything previously learnt that it will take some time to get used to it. Notice the final position (fig. 213e) which is referred to as 'back support'.

The forward seat circle

From back support the gymnast lifts on to her hands and takes her hips backwards. She then takes her nose to her knees. (Most gymnasts start this movement with the thumbs round the bar and move them back only when they begin the circle.) The gymnast must stay in the pike as she circles forwards (fig. 214b). Notice in fig. 214c that the backs of the knees are over the bar but when the gymnast finishes the circle her hips are over the bar (fig. 214d).

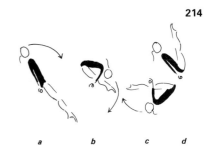

214

a   b   c   d

The upstart

This movement, referred to as the 'kip' in American books, is the key to success on bars. There are many types of upstarts and it is important that the gymnast not only does these movements but also learns how to swing out of the upstart into another movement without an extra swing. It may take the gymnast several months to master this complex skill.

Firstly the coach must decide whether or not the gymnast is strong enough to learn this movement. If she can do at least five leg lifts (see page 23) correctly then she should manage.

The float or glide

This must be learnt first. The gymnast stands as shown in fig. 215a. Notice that the feet are just in front of the hips and that there is a straight line through the arms and back. She then bends the knees slightly, taking care that the knees do not move in front of the toes. She must then jump backwards still keeping the straight line through the arms and back. It may help if the coach holds the gymnast by the hips to pull her backwards as she jumps. She then swings forwards to her fullest stretch. As she swings forwards her feet should remain a constant distance from the floor, approximately 10 cms. Having reached this position the gymnast should then swing back to the starting position keeping the legs straight and just off the ground as before. This tests whether or not the gymnast has enough strength in her hip flexors to keep her feet off the floor. Having practised that several times she then needs to go through the action of an upstart.

Using a broomstick or a spare bar the gymnast can practise as shown in fig. 216, by lying on the ground. She lifts her legs over bringing the toes to the bar. She then gradually sits up pulling the bar down the front of the

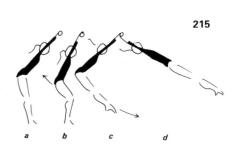

215

a   b   c   d

leg. In order to bring the bar right into the groin she must bend her arms. This position (fig. 216d) will be exactly the same when done on the bar as the swing-in ready for a swing-away (figs 207b and 217d). The gymnast must realize the importance of this position.

Once this is well established, the gymnast should then attempt the upstart between the bars (fig. 217). The bars should be placed at the correct width; when the gymnast is at full stretch the bar should be just at the bottom of the gluteals. The coach will need to stand in for the first attempts. Place a horse, box or similar object between the bars to stand on, its height depending on the height of the coach. The coach's near hand may need to aid the movement of the legs but the other hand must be free to put in the middle of the back to help push the hips to the bar. In the beginning the coach will do a lot of pushing and shoving because the gymnast will not understand this complex movement. After some time, though, little or no support should be needed.

216

217

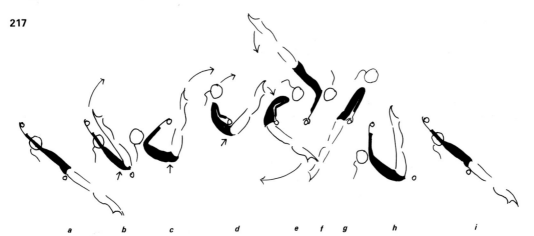

a   b   c   d   e f g   h   i

Notice in fig. 217d that the gymnast has the bar into the groin and from here she just continues to circle forwards to come to the classic position of preparation (front support). From here the gymnast should swing away and return to the bar with a straight body and then pike under the bar keeping the hips to the bar for a little while before allowing them to come to the low bar. The legs should then be lowered (figs 217h and i) to repeat the upstart. The upstart can be used as a single element in a bar exercise, taking the gymnast from the bottom bar to the top, as an introduction to upstarts, or as a method of increasing stamina which will prove very useful at a later stage. In all these repetitions the legs must be kept together and straight. If necessary tie the gymnast's ankles together.

Once the gymnast has established this pattern and is nearly able to do the skill by herself then the float can be added to it. By learning the movement between the bars the gymnast is able to concentrate on the upstart section and not worry about the float. The gymnast can start with

218

a   b   c   d   e   g   f   h   j i

her hands on the bar, as she did in the learning of the float, or if she is competent she can start away from the bar as shown in fig. 218. She should start with her arms behind her as shown and then, as she jumps forwards to catch the bar, her arms swing forwards and upwards. Ensure that she still gets this feeling of jumping the hips back and stretching through the shoulders. A common fault is that the gymnast lifts the hands too high so that they drop on to the bar. She should aim for the centre of the bar. At the end of the float she must extend so that the whole body lifts as near to the horizontal as possible. She then goes through the upstart action as she did between the bars. The toes must still come to the bar and the bar be pulled up the front of the legs. Notice again the position in fig. 218h before she circles forwards to bring her to the final position from which she can swing to handstand or straddle on or whatever is required in a voluntary exercise. The coach can follow her through this movement making a platform with her hands in the float (one hand on the gymnast's back and one on the back of the thighs). When following her through the upstart stage make sure her movement isn't restricted; be ready to move under the bar and back again. There are two important things to remember if you want success in this movement: the gymnast must be strong, and she must understand the movement. Go through it on paper first, studying fig. 218 for each position in the sequence.

The gymnast must swing away at the end of the upstart; this can be directed into a back hip circle or straddle on or squat through.

Fig. 219a shows a common fault in the upstart. From this front rest position the gymnast then has to swing the legs back under the bar in order to go into another movement; she will therefore have an extra swing in an exercise, which means losing marks. The only movement that she can do from the front support is a forward hip circle (fig. 209) which leads well into other movements. The only problem is that if she has a voluntary exercise that is always composed of upstart forward circle she will lose marks for repetition and poor technical value. She will also be in trouble if a set exercise demands something else.

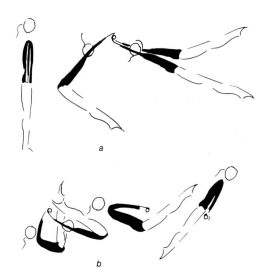

a

b

219

The long upstart

This movement (fig. 220) comes from the low bar with the gymnast facing the high bar. It can come from back support as shown, which could be arrived at by doing a forward seat circle or a float two-feet squat through upstart. Initiation into the float is rather limited. The gymnast must try and let the legs swing down to the vertical before swinging them forwards. At the end of the float the gymnast needs considerable strength and body tension to get to such a position as shown, before piking into the upstart. The end of the movement is as for the previous upstarts.

Later on the gymnast may do the long upstart from a hip beat straddle or stoop-over.

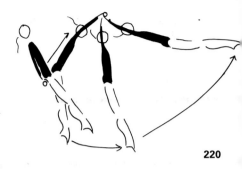

220

The short upstart

This is an upstart which has no float. In fig. 221 the gymnast is shown coming from an upstart to catch the top bar or a mount jump to the top bar. From the back swing shown in position fig. 221a the gymnast lifts the

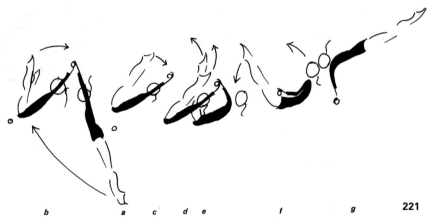

b   a   c   d   e   f   g   **221**

legs through straddle to a piked position. The toes are brought in close to the bar and then the upstart happens as before. The gymnast must be very strong in the hip flexors to lift the toes to the bar and maintain this position for rather longer than normal (fig. 221d). As always, swing is vital; without it there is only one substitute, brute strength, which is an undesirable factor. This movement can also come from half a back seat circle as shown in fig. 222.

The upstart to catch

This movement takes the gymnast from the low bar to the high bar; a very useful skill when composing a bar exercise. The gymnast performs an ordinary float upstart; this must be good for her to achieve the catch. The toes must go to the bar as normal and the bar be pulled down the thigh. The gymnast releases her hands from the low bar and reaches up to catch the high bar. The coach can give her more confidence in the beginning by

a   b   c   d   e

222

supporting under the thigh and middle of the back as indicated by the arrows in fig. 223c. Having caught the bar the gymnast must swing the legs well back so that she is able to move into the next skill easily.

A common fault here is that the gymnast becomes anxious and releases her hands from the low bar too soon and falls. She must think about finishing the upstart action; that is pulling the bar up the legs. Distance between the bars is fairly important when doing this skill; a small gymnast is obviously going to find it difficult to catch the top bar if the bars are very wide. If the bar distance is not limited by any other movements don't make the mistake of having the bars very close; this restricts the amount of swing that is possible and the work becomes static instead of flowing and swinging.

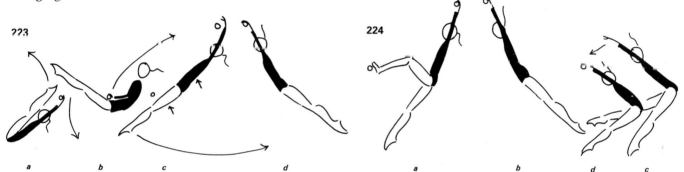

The drop to low bar
As with the previous skill this movement (fig. 224) is very useful when working out a bar exercise. In fact the two can be combined together to make a good training exercise; upstart to catch, drop float and upstart to catch, etc.

This movement is not difficult but it does require good timing and strength in the hip flexors. In order to practise this the gymnast needs to initiate a swing as shown in figs 224a and b. The gymnast pushes away from the low bar to swing back. From this swing back the gymnast pikes the body, bringing the feet forwards. In the piked position the gymnast drops to the low bar. First of all the gymnast can practise the swing back to pike and then swing back again and pike. This whip-like action is important as it will be useful for more advanced moves later.

If a crash mat is placed under the low bar the gymnast can practise this skill by herself as she must find the right timing. In figs 224c and d the legs are straddled. This makes the movement slightly easier, as not so much effort is needed by the hip flexors. The legs should be joined together by the end of the float and before going into the upstart.

The float squat two feet through uprise
The float is the same as before with the gymnast stretching well through the shoulders at the end of the float. The last part of the movement can

first be learnt on the floor with a broomstick (fig. 225). From lying on her back the gymnast pikes, bringing the feet underneath the bar and then pulls the bar down the back of the legs to come to V sit. Obviously the more supple the gymnast is in the hamstrings, the tighter her pike or fold. It is important to get a good horizontal position at the end of the float. When trying the whole skill on the bar (fig. 226) there is often a desire to hollow over the bar. This is incorrect; the gymnast must maintain the V position as it will aid her when moving into the next skill.

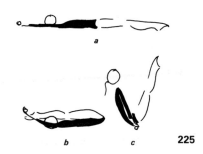

225

The float straddle cut to catch

The float should be performed as described in the float upstart and the legs are brought into the body at the end of the first swing (fig. 227a). The fold should be tight with the shins pressed well to the face. In the float two feet through, the pike gradually opens but in this case the pike must stay well folded until the gymnast has circled so that her arms are horizontal and she is able to press down on the bar with her hands. At this height in the swing she should straddle her legs, letting go of the bar and then re-grasping again once the legs have straddled. The legs remain straddled on the re-grasping and the gymnast should then carry on into a float and probably an upstart. The logical teaching progression is to learn the float upstart; then the float squat two feet through to back support and then the straddle cut. In the beginning stages the gymnast need not worry about re-grasping but simply straddle before landing on the feet on the floor. If the gymnast needs any support the coach should lift from behind and support the gymnast round the waist as she straddles (fig. 228). The action for straddling the legs is to open them out to the side as much as possible without any forward movement. This gives the gymnast plenty of clearance from the bar.

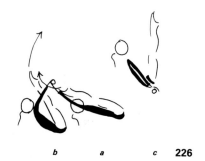

226

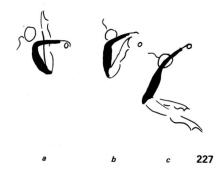

227

228

The back upstart

This complicated movement is easier to learn if the uprise movement and the backward seat circle have been mastered. It is a combination of the two skills. The position shown in fig. 229c can be learnt on the floor. From

Above A straddle over after a hip beat showing good height (Muchina, USSR).

Left The gymnast is so confident when changing her grasp in a forward sole circle that she does so before the feet have straddled on (Dando, GB).

the extended shoulder position the gymnast lets the legs drop to come to a piked inverted hang. She then circles backwards to come to back support (fig. 229f). In the beginning the gymnast will probably be low on the upwards extension as shown in fig. 229c. Encourage the gymnast to increase her height as this will improve the backward seat circle and will also increase the technical value of the movement. Although this skill is not used a great deal it does provide an interesting combination to any bar exercise. Its lack of use is probably due to its complexity.

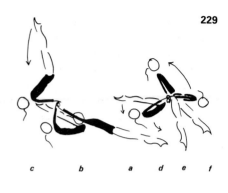

229

c b a d e f

The straddle on and underswing dismount

This movement can be learnt fairly early in the gymnast's career but it does need a lot of attention as it will lead on to many more advanced skills.

First the gymnast needs to practise the straddle on. This can be done on the floor or on a single floor bar (fig. 230). From a front support position the gymnast straddles the feet either side of the hands. The feet should be close to the hands nearly touching them. If your gymnast is doing this on the floor, then draw a line to represent the bar. Make sure that the gymnast has got her feet in line with the hands on the imaginary bar. Once she has straddled on the 'bar' look at the hands and you will see that they are on top of the bar. When she circles back under the bar she will need to put her hands further forwards round the bar in order to get a better grip. When she has placed her hands 'under the bar' she should then lift up on to the toes in order to get the hips as far away from the bar as possible. She should press the shoulders into the thighs and keep the head down. If a suitable mat is placed behind the gymnast she can then fall backwards.

230

When doing this on the bars this movement should be exactly the same. She starts in front support and prepares by swinging the legs under the bar and then swinging back and upwards. The swing-away must be high in order for the gymnast to get the hips high. When the gymnast is balanced for a moment on the bar she then has to release her grip and put her hands further round the bar (fig. 231). She then swings backwards pulling on the hands and pushing down with the feet into the bar. Just before her body comes to the horizontal on the other side of the bar she takes her feet off the bar and extends her legs upwards. She must extend the whole of her body, letting go of the bar, to travel upwards and forwards before landing. The body should be straight with the gymnast reaching out with her feet for the landing.

231

With the first attempts the gymnast will probably need support. By now the gymnast should be fairly competent at straddling on to the bar. If she is not too sure support her from the front as shown in fig. 232.

Now the coach will need to stand at the side and in front of the bar. The nearest hand goes under the bar to hold the gymnast's wrist and the far hand goes under the bar to hold the gymnast's ankle (figs 233 and 234).

232

When the gymnast circles under the bar the coach should have the gymnast perfectly secure as shown in the diagram. When she extends the legs outwards the coach should then release the legs and just hold the wrist until the gymnast has landed. It is very important that the coach insists on the correct technique being performed. A common fault is that the gymnast puts her instep on the bar instead of the ball of the foot.

The Americans call this move (fig. 235) a 'toe on shoot' because the toes and ball of the foot are placed on the bar.

233

234

235

The straddle and underswing with half turn

Having perfected the undershoot the gymnast can try the movement with a half turn so that she stays on the bar. This can be practised on the low bar. As the gymnast extends the feet upwards and outwards she takes one hand off and moves it across to the other side of the second hand. This now means that her hands are in mixed grasp (fig. 236a). The coach will need to stand in for first attempts. She should stand in on the side away from the gymnast's turn; if the gymnast turns to the left the coach will stand on her right side. As the gymnast extends her legs upwards and outwards the coach will place her arms underneath the gymnast's body so that one arm is under the abdomen and one under the thighs. When the coach is not there the gymnast will have to pike in to come on to the feet. This movement can then be taken to the top bar. When the gymnast has learnt to hip beat she can do the turn over the low bar.

The hand change can be done with both hands changing together. This is more difficult but better for the gymnast as she does not have to worry about changing the other hand later. As the gymnast makes the half turn so she will release both hands together to re-grasp in ordinary grasp (fig. 236b). The coach will stand in as before. This movement can be developed to a more difficult skill by opening the arms before re-grasping. This was performed by Tourischeva but has not really been equalled by any other gymnast.

a

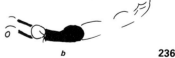

b

236

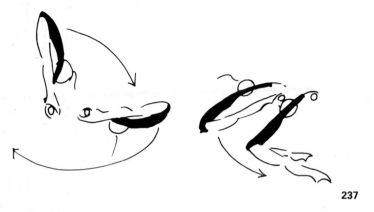

237

The straddle on forward sole circle and float

The gymnast straddles on as before except that she needs to place her instep on the bar. As she arrives on the bar with her feet she has to change her over grasp to reverse under grasp (fig. 237). She then circles forwards. When her back reaches the horizontal on the other side of the bar she must change to over grasp, taking the feet off the bar and keeping her legs straddled and piked. She is then ready to go into the float for an upstart. There is no efficient way of standing in for this movement. If the gymnast understands the back sole circle well then she should be safe with this movement. A crash mat can be placed under the bar. If the gymnast does not manage the move she just brings her feet to the ground.

238

Movements from hip beat

The coach must first of all find the correct bar distance for the gymnast. The gymnast should go into a hanging position as shown in fig. 238. From the swing-in of the legs the gymnast then swings the legs backwards and upwards to lie away off the low bar. When the gymnast returns to the bar, coming in straight, she allows the body to pike on impact. Obviously, if the bar is in the wrong position for the gymnast then this is painful. The bar should be just above the pubic region and resting in the groin. When training the gymnast is well advised to put two foam rubber squares across her hips inside her leotard, or in her track suit trousers or tights, to stop her getting too bruised.

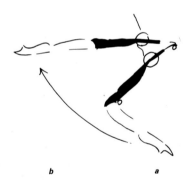

b   *a*

The hip beat from low bar

The beat from the bar shown in fig. 239 should be practised many times before developing the movement. In the swing-away (fig. 239b) the gymnast should be straight, lifting her stomach high above the bar. The coach may need to assist here by lifting the gymnast on each swing-away under the stomach. The coach should stand between the bars for this.

c   *d*   **239**

Above The hecht from long swing used as a bar dismount. After the initial lift off the low bar the arms are brought to the sides to increase rotation before landing (Tourischeva, USSR).

Left Good shoulder mobility is necessary in the wrap to catch to achieve an early grasp and create a good after swing (Dando, GB).

Having mastered this action the gymnast should try it from a squat position on the low bar (fig. 240), pushing off the feet and throwing the legs out behind her, keeping a good stretch in the shoulders. The hip beat can then be done from the long swing (see below).

240

The hip beat straddle over the low bar

Another useful linking movement. As the gymnast rises above the bar in her lay away she should straddle her legs and pike the body to swing forward over the low bar (fig. 241). Again, she should try and keep a straight line through her arms on the swing forward so that she does not drop or jolt in the shoulders.

241

The hip beat swing-away to low bar

Fig. 242 shows a simple development of the hip beat. As the gymnast arrives above the bar she lets go of the top bar to pike backwards and grasp the low bar, swinging into a float with legs straddled or together.

The long swing

This is a movement (fig. 243) that is often taught inadequately. It is regarded as a simple movement, and is therefore not given sufficient thought and performed badly.

From front support on the top bar the preparation is almost the same as for a backward circle. Whereas in the backward circle preparation the shoulders were kept forward, here the shoulders are allowed to swing away with the body. The body is kept straight, with the head held in a normal position and the arms kept straight the whole time. To throw back the head will give too much hollow in the back and result in loss of control. If the shoulders are not taken far enough back in the swing-away, then in the swing down the arms will have to bend; a pronounced angle

242

243

between chest and arms will be needed if this occurs and this will kill the swing (the flexion in the shoulder region will have to extend and therefore drop the body). This movement should first be tried on the low bar with the coach holding the gymnast under the hips. The coach should guide the gymnast so that she feels the swing out over the bar with the shoulders moving back.

The long swing wrap to catch

This movement can be quite frightening at first attempt if the coach does not take the gymnast through the correct progression.

1 From long swing the gymnast should swing into the low bar and allow the legs to wrap round the bar so the bar is in the groin and the toes are forced as near to the gymnast's face as possible (fig. 244). The gymnast should be able to feel her hands almost being pulled off the top bar and the two bars being pulled slightly closer together due to the wrapping action.

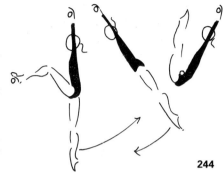

244

2 The gymnast should jump from the floor with support from the coach to catch the top bar in dislocated grasp, the arms stretched obliquely upwards and the hands turned out so that the palms face the high bar (fig. 245). This should be done several times for familiarization of the grasp.

3 From a lying position over the low bar, as shown in fig. 246, the gymnast, assisted by the coach, swings up and back to catch the top bar in dislocated grasp. The coach stands between the bars and supports with the arm nearest the top bar round the gymnast's thighs and the arm nearest the low bar under the gymnast's stomach (this arm goes under the low bar).

245

If the coach is at all unsure of the gymnast's awareness of this movement then she should go through the progressions until completely familiar.

The coach should stand in between the bars; it may help, if there are crash mats available, to have one under the low bar. To do the complete movement (fig. 247) the gymnast should do a long swing as previously; she hits the bar straight and pikes round immediately hanging on with her hands until she feels they must come off the top bar. The legs at this stage should be well past the vertical and nearly to the horizontal; the body and arms then should swing free and rapidly in a backward circle to swing upwards and backwards to grasp the high bar in dislocated grasp. The legs should drop to about 45 degrees below the horizontal as the back muscles contract and lift the upper body backwards in an arch. The coach takes her arm round the gymnast's thighs before she comes off the bar

246

247

and helps lift under the stomach when she is free of the bar. At a later stage the coach may find it easier to lift the gymnast just about from the waist as she reaches backwards to grasp the top bar; this is also less restricting for the gymnast. Several men coaches use this support, but it may not be suitable for all women coaches.

A common fault is for the gymnast to let go of the top bar too soon and 'bump' around the bar; she may not create enough tension between the two bars through letting go of the top bar too soon or not swinging the legs rapidly enough round the low bar. In the lift away there is a tendency on first attempts to be straight or piked due to lack of tension in the gluteals. If the gymnast is very stiff-shouldered she is going to find this movement difficult as she will have to take her arms very wide in order to get any backward extension. It may be, therefore, that success will only be achieved by some gymnasts if they spend some time loosening their shoulders.

The swing to handstand

It is quite difficult for a gymnast to include a handstand in her routine but she can start to learn this very necessary move quite early on.

Provided the gymnast has a good lay-away ready for straddles and squats then she should be ready to learn the handstand. Firstly, the coach should see how far in fact the gymnast can get on her lay-away (fig. 248).

Having established that this is fair and that there is no loss of control then the next stage can be attempted. The coach should place a box or similar piece of apparatus under the low bar (fig. 249). The coach will then stand astride the bar with the gymnast close to her in front support. The

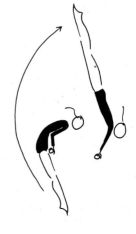

248

249

coach will support under the nearest shoulder and be ready with the other hand to lift the thigh. The preparation before the swing-away will need to be deep with the shoulders well forwards and the gymnast well piked. As she aims to swing to handstand the coach will keep hold of the shoulder allowing the natural movement to happen and also help to lift the thighs. As the gymnast gets nearer the handstand so the shoulders should move backwards to come above the hands. The coach may need to guide this movement on first attempts. Notice that the gymnast is straight in the handstand. If the gymnast lacks control and cannot achieve a straight handstand on the floor then she should not be trying this movement.

Having reached the handstand the gymnast obviously has to come down. Still holding the shoulder and thigh the coach aids the gymnast as she takes the shoulders forwards and lowers the body, bringing the hips into the bar. After some practice the gymnast should manage this action by herself.

In a voluntary exercise one of the options, in coming out of a handstand, is for the gymnast to long swing; another is for the gymnast to half turn and then long swing. This can be practised quite simply on a single floor bar (fig. 250). The gymnast steps to handstand on the bar and makes a half turn by taking one hand across so that she is in mixed grasp. She then falls on to the crash mat keeping the body straight. She must have good body tension. The hand change is important so a lot of practice at this level is helpful. Having succeeded in changing one hand the gymnast should then turn the second hand round so as she goes into long swing to fall on the mat both hands are in over grasp. The gymnast may wish to change her hands another way, by turning the hand on the pivoting side first and then taking the other one across to complete the turn. The hand changes must be completed as soon as possible, well before the gymnast hits the mat.

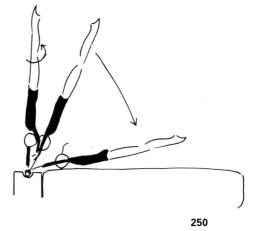

250

Obviously the gymnast must be very skilled in the handstand and turn before attempting this on the high bar; the pull on the hands is very powerful so she must be well aware of what she is doing.

Dismounts

The back circle 'hecht'
This skill is mostly used as a dismount but can be used within a bar exercise. The word *hecht* is German for pike. The movement of flight off the bar is created from a piked circle round the bar. Many gymnasts have problems learning this circle as they are so skilled at doing a backward hip circle with a straight body but now they have to be piked and bring the bar into the groin. The gymnast lays away from the bar but needs to be slightly hollow in this action (fig. 251a). This creates greater speed in the circle and therefore increases the flight off the bar. From the hollow

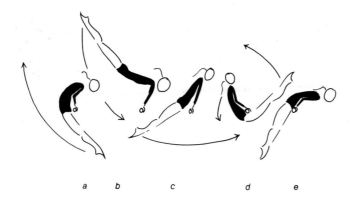

a　　*b*　　　*c*　　　　*d*　　　*e*　　　　**251**

lay-away the hips must come in to meet the bar; the feet are brought rapidly under the bar. The gymnast should practise the back circle on its own many times. The arms will have to bend slightly to allow the bar into the groin. At the end of the circle she should have enough speed to fall away from the bar or to begin to circle around again (fig. 251e). From the piked position the gymnast now needs to practise the opening action. This should be practised first of all on a box top with the coach holding the thighs. From hanging over the box the gymnast must lift the head and shoulders rapidly, maintaining tension throughout the body. The arms should stay by the imaginary bar at the gymnast's side.

Having established the shape pattern the gymnast can then try the whole skill. She will circle backwards as before. A crash mat needs to be placed in front of the low bar. As she sees the mat then the gymnast needs to open the body to lift off the bar (fig. 252). The coach will need to support under the abdomen and across the back. The gymnast may knock her shins on the first attempts so it is advisable that she wears her tracksuit trousers. The timing of the movement will be a matter of trial and error for the gymnast. Obviously, if she dives into the ground she is coming off too soon, or if she tends to over-rotate then she is coming off too late.

When finally learnt this dismount is usually done from the top bar in either direction. Outwards has less fear attached to it than going over the low bar.

The long swing 'hecht'

The same movement as above can be done from a long swing. This is easier and can only be done from the low bar. It does, however, create problems if the gymnast is small and has been working the bars wide for non-wrapping movements. As with the hip beat skills and the wrap to catch, the bars must be at a precise distance to fit the gymnast's physique.

If the gymnast has already learnt the wrap to catch then this should be very easy to learn. She should not learn the two moves together as she is likely to get confused with the timing of both. In the wrap to catch she will open the body when she is approximately horizontal. For the *hecht* she will start lifting the body at about 45 degrees or when she sees the mat in front of her (fig. 252). She must create tension between the bars as for the wrap to catch by holding on to the top bar and pulling the two bars together by the strong wrapping action.

The coach will stand in as for the back circle *hecht* (fig. 253). It is easier to lift the gymnast up off the bar as the arms are forwards and as the hands never touch the low bar. It is important that the coach gets her hand on the back before the gymnast leaves the bar.

The swing and back somersault off

This movement is usually proceded by a squat or straddle over the low bar with the hands on the top bar. The squat or straddle over is taken from a hip beat. As the body comes over the bar the feet must pass as close to the low bar as possible, extending the shoulders. The forward swing is continued to its maximum when the gymnast lifts the feet and knees to tuck, taking the legs between the arms, releasing her grasp and back somersaulting off (fig. 254). The coach can assist on top of the arm and help lift the hips on the forward swing. This movement is easily performed, but the somersault is often made just under the top bar. Maximum swing must be achieved in order that the somersault is well away from the bar and as high as possible.

252

253

254

Further Information

Apparatus specifications for competitions

1 *Floor* 12 m × 12 m. This is a sprung area stipulated by the Federation Internationale de Gymnastique. This is very expensive to buy, so many gym clubs have a matted area only.
2 *Beam* Length 500 cms; depth 16 cms; width 10 cms; height from floor 120 cms. For some junior and regional competitions the beam may be lower.
3 *Asymmetric bars* Height (top bar) 230 cms, (low bar) 150 cms. Horizontal distance between the bars must be adjustable (55–90 cms).
4 *Vaulting horse* Height 120 cms. For some junior and regional competitions the height may vary.
5 *Spring-board* This must be of a reuther type. Check with the apparatus manufacturer.

The BAGA

The British Amateur Gymnastics Association governs the sport of gymnastics in the United Kingdom. Their address is 95 High Street, Slough, Berks SL1 1DH. This organization runs two gymnastic schemes for girls: the *Sunday Times* Award and the Gold Top Award. The National Development Scheme for Girls is a series of set work competitions; this scheme is essential for the potential competitive gymnast.

Suggested reading

The Gymnast (BAGA magazine)
The International Gymnast Magazine (available from Sherwood House, Hinckley Road, Burbage, Leics LE10 2AG)
J. Coulton *Women's Gymnastics* (E. P. Sport, 1977)
Janet Fidler and Brian Steele *Olympic Gymnastics for Girls* (John Sherratt & Son Limited, 1976)
Jim and Pauline Prestidge *Your Book of Gymnastics* (Faber and Faber, 1964)
P. Prestidge *Better Gymnastics* (Kaye & Ward, 1977)
P. Prestidge *Women's Gymnastics for Performer and Coach* (Faber & Faber, 1972)
Peter Tatlow (ed.) *Gymnastics* (Lyric Books, 1979)